THE PANTHEON

William L. MacDonald

THE PANTHEON

DESIGN, MEANING, AND PROGENY

HARVARD UNIVERSITY PRESS
CAMBRIDGE, MASSACHUSETTS

for Nicholas and Noel

1. The Emperor Hadrian.

ACKNOWLEDGEMENTS

My debt to Hugh Honour and John Fleming, the editors of this series, is a pleasure to record. They very kindly asked me to write on the Pantheon, and their skillful editing greatly improved my work. I learned a good deal from their criticisms and corrections, and from several articles and books they referred me to. For all this I am most grateful indeed.

Several friends and acquaintances generously discussed different aspects of the subject with me; their names are given, with warmest thanks, in the appropriate places. Barbara Satz read the manuscript with painstaking care, exposing vague and infelicitous passages, and I want to thank her for her patient, productive help. I am also much indebted to Francesca and Jon Wiig for their generous support of my work through the Dean William Emerson Fund.

Permission to reprint copyrighted material has been given by George Braziller, Inc., Farrar, Straus & Giroux, Inc., the Harvard University Press, the Princeton University Press, and Verlag Ernst Wasmuth in Tübingen. The Frontispiece appears with the permission of the National Gallery in Washington (the Samuel H. Kress Collection). The sources for the other illustrations are given in the list thereof.

Northampton, Massachusetts　　　　　　　　　　　　　　　*W.L.M.*
September 1973

1

IN THE TEMPLE
OF THE
WHOLE WORLD

Hadrian's Pantheon is one of the grand architectural creations of all time: original, utterly bold, many-layered in associations and meaning, the container of a kind of immanent universality. It speaks of an even wider world than that of imperial Rome, and has left its stamp upon architecture more than any other building. Its message, compounded of mystery and fact, of stasis and mutability, of earth and that above, pulses through the architecture of western man; its progeny, in both shape and idea, are all about. The force of its presence and its planetary symbolism still works irresistibly upon the visitor who, passing through the bronze doors into the enclosing rotunda, experiences the awesome reach of its canopied void [Title page].

Did Hadrian and his architects intend all this? Is it possible to be specific and convincing about such things? At present the answer to these questions is both yes and no. The far-reaching influence of the Pantheon upon subsequent architecture is undeniable, and is documented for both design and certain aspects of meaning; scholars and architects have worked a good deal on these problems. As for Hadrian, we can warrant his brilliance and his deep interest in architecture, as well as the audacity and sophistication of his architects. And it can clearly be shown that the conception and design of the building were original. But although there is a fair amount of data, the ultimate meaning of the Pantheon remains, in its complexity, enigmatic. That each of us tends to make of his subjective experience of the building what he will is a measure of the depth and universality of its message.

The pages that follow contain both fact and speculation, in an attempt to describe Hadrian's potent creation and to estimate its meaning and significance. Facts are given first: the evidence for dating, a brief life-history of the building, and a description of its parts and structure. The principles and historical background of its architectural design are then discussed. There follows a reconnaissance of several levels of meaning and symbolism; and the book finishes with an assessment of the catalytic role of the Pantheon in the history of architecture.

The architect of the Pantheon is unknown. Almost certainly it was not Hadrian himself, though his name has been suggested. A thoroughgoing professional would have had to make the drawings and models, calculate all details of design and construction, and supervise the complicated, exacting work as it progressed. But whoever the architect may have been, Hadrian's building it was and is; he stands in relation to it as Justinian to the Hagia Sophia or Louis XIV to Versailles. Hadrian, the Pantheon, and the cultural texture of the early second century are all inextricably interwoven, and there can be no doubt that the conception of the building and the motivating personality behind its creation were Hadrian's.

He was born in Roman Spain of an established colonial family during the reign of the emperor Vespasian in the year 76.* He served successfully in a variety of government posts, chiefly military, and was given preference by his kinsman the emperor Trajan (reigned 98–117); when Trajan died Hadrian became emperor. He was a deeply cultivated man, at home with all things Greek, a multi-faceted yet apparently restless and rather difficult person, who nevertheless seems to have borne his heavy responsibilities well [1]. There may have been elements of genius in him; at the least he was exceptionally intelligent and accomplished in a number of different activities — administrative and military matters, of course, but also poetry, painting, and architecture. If an ancient view of his nature is reliable, it is no wonder that his contemporaries failed to warm to him:

> He was, in the same person, austere and genial, dignified and playful, dilatory and quick to act, niggardly and generous, deceitful and straightforward, cruel and merciful, and always in all things changeable (*et semper in omnibus varius*).

An aspect of his apparent willfulness was the omission of his name from some of the imperial inscriptions put up on public buildings erected or renovated round the Empire during his reign (117–38), a most un-emperorlike thing to do. Where the Pantheon stands there had been an earlier, rectangular sanctuary of the same dedication,

*The designation 'A.D.' is not used here, though 'B.C.' is.

12

built by Augustus' great minister Agrippa and dedicated about 25 B.C. That building, twice burned before Hadrian's accession, was entirely replaced by him with the present structure. Yet he restored Agrippa's original inscription on his new building: M·AGRIPPA·L·F·COS· TERTIVM·FECIT – Marcus Agrippa the son of Lucius, three times consul, built this [2]. Considerable confusion has resulted from this inscription. Even now, the Pantheon is not infrequently said to have been built in the time of Augustus Caesar – a date wide of the mark by a century and a half – because of the inscription in bold bronze letters (they are modern, but faithfully reproduce Hadrian's) that spreads across the entablature of the great porch.

The correct date is the first half of Hadrian's reign. The building was *Date* not begun before 117, and was probably dedicated about 126–8. During the second century, Roman brickmakers methodically stamped a proportion of their large, tile-shaped bricks [3] with the names of their brickyards and of the consuls currently in office, or with similarly datable information. Some of the bricks in every consignment were pressed with wooden stamps before firing, perhaps for purposes of inventory or taxation. It was done when the clay was still comparatively wet and soft, and in this fashion a lot of information was recorded in abbreviated Latin. In our own time epigraphers, specialists in inscriptions, have carefully studied very large numbers of these stamps, which can be seen in the actual buildings, in fallen structures, during modern restoration and repair, and the like. As we know the dates the annual consuls were in office, we can date bricks bearing consuls' names. Frequently dates can also be obtained from other information yielded by stamps – the names of master potters, of brick-yards, or the shape and design of the stamp itself – because of the accumulation of interrelated data in this discipline. As a result, the work of architectural historians and archaeologists in dating imperial buildings is sometimes much simplified. Brick-stamps establish a *terminus post quem*, since the building in whose structure they are found could not have been built before the earliest dates recorded on them. And through the knowledge of Roman imperial building practices that has gradually been accumulated, it is often possible to estimate within fairly narrow limits the time between manufacture and use. In the body of the Pantheon there is a preponderance of brick-stamps of the early 120s, and it is upon this fact, more than any other, that the dating of the building is based.

But there is other useful information. Analysis of style and architectural design, in the story of the evolution of Roman architecture, is crucial, and it will be made in a later chapter. But it should be said here that the conception, scale, and technology of the Pantheon [4] can be shown to have been the product of their time, datable steps in that evolution. It is also significant that Hadrian, after an absence on a tour of inspection of the provinces that had lasted several years, was in or near Rome in 125–8; perhaps the Pantheon was dedicated toward the end of that period. Hadrian's own chief architectural creation, the huge Temple of Venus and Rome [5], was begun after the Pantheon, in 121, and not finished until 136 or 137.

A final word about dating. There are those who have held that the columned, temple-like porch is related to the domed rotunda in such an inept way that the two parts must differ in date [6 and 7]. The porch may be Agrippa's, it has been said, for after all the inscription clearly says so. The argument continues that Hadrian came along and gracelessly attached his new rotunda to the earlier porch [8]. Sometimes this supposed inelegance is adduced as evidence of Hadrian's own amateurishness in architecture, that is, it has been claimed that he designed the whole building, but because he was an amateur he could not adjust the two parts satisfactorily – a strange kind of argument, that gives him great talent and then takes it away. We will see that in this marriage of temple front and domed rotunda an entirely new idea was being tried, and because of this some elements of design are not as finished in their visual and decorative effects as they might otherwise be. Also, there were sound reasons for regarding the juncture of the major parts as a relatively insignificant aspect of the whole design. All these matters will be discussed more fully in the chapter on architectural design. It need only be said that the temple-front porch, the domed rotunda, and the blocky form interposed between them are beyond any doubt all of Hadrianic date [9].

Apart from its actual construction, the most important fact about the physical existence of the Pantheon is that about the year 609, in the depths of the Dark Ages, the emperor in Constantinople gave permission for Pope Boniface IV to consecrate it as a church, Sancta Maria ad Martyres, 'after the pagan filth was removed'. Rome by then had shrunk to little more than a village, but this renewal of a pagan temple as a Christian church, highly significant as an act of care by the impoverished Romans for the monumental relics of their momentous past, went a long way toward insuring the Pantheon's survival. Its conversion into a church placed it under whatever program of maintenance the papal town could provide. However crude this work may from time to time have been, the minimum necessary was done. And if Byzantine emperors and popes themselves now and then removed its bronze and gilded fittings, the excellence of its

2. The Pantheon, north façade.

3. The Pantheon, detail of the rotunda exterior.

4. The Pantheon, analytical drawing.
5. The Temple of Venus and Rome, Rome.

6. The Pantheon,
junction of the intermediate block
with the rotunda.

7. The Pantheon, east side.

8. The Pantheon, porch.

Hadrianic construction and the efforts over the centuries of drain-cleaners and rooters-out of trees and vegetation combined to preserve it until proper help was brought in modern times. As a result it stands, by far the best-preserved of all monumental Roman buildings.

During the five centuries between its construction and its consecration as a church, many of the public buildings and squares nearby, and all over Rome, fell into ruin. The removal of the capital of the Empire to Constantinople in 330 was a heavy blow to the city in many ways. The well-organized imperial offices of works, which had been amply supplied with men and money, all but ceased to function. At the very end of the century, about 398, the absent imperial government found it necessary to issue a prohibition, on pain of exile, against building huts or hovels in the once so grand Campus Martius, the flattish district in the bend of the Tiber where the Pantheon stands. The dilapidation of buildings large and small, by both man and nature, together with flooding and the near cessation of the city's sanitation and other public services, caused the level of the ground around the Pantheon gradually to rise [2 and 10]. This was an important event in the transformation of the appearance and architectural effect of the building, as important as the loss of its adjoining structures. Because of this period in the history of Rome, the Pantheon looks as if it had settled into the ground. Not at all; the ground has risen, and risen considerably, around it.

The building gradually became known to the Romans as Santa Maria Rotonda, its popular designation to this day. The Byzantine emperor Constans II robbed it of its gilded bronze roof tiles during a short visit to Rome in 663, but he seems shortly afterwards to have lost them in Sicily to Arab corsairs. Meanwhile the building was altered by cutting passages through one of the great piers by the south apse [11], in ignorance of its structural function, and it may be that cartloads of martyrs' bones were brought to the new church from the catacombs. A new lead covering was placed over the Hadrianic concrete dome, probably in the eighth century. This covering received much attention during the Renaissance [12 and 13]. A number of inscribed lead plates are still in place on the dome, among them some with the arms and titles of the great humanist pope, Nicholas V (1447–55). A bell tower was added above the center of the façade, on the porch roof, in the late thirteenth century [10], and from time to time other ephemeral constructions appeared on the intermediate block. In 1520 Raphael, at his choice, was buried in the rotunda under the temple front or aedicula at position 6 [11]. In the early seventeenth century twin towers were erected at the ends of the intermediate block, the work perhaps of Gianlorenzo Bernini but more probably of Carlo Maderno; they were dismantled in the 1880s [14]. These particular additions to the Pantheon had considerable influence on subsequent classicizing architecture.

Many woodcuts, map representations, etchings, and drawings of the building show these various transformations in its appearance. Shops and booths appeared, especially between the porch columns; these were suppressed in Renaissance times. In antiquity the space in front of the building to the north had been an elongated, paved court framed by colonnades [15 and 16].* In time the colonnades disappeared, the level of the ground rose considerably, and buildings appeared over a fair portion of the site of the ancient forecourt. From the sixteenth century onward the abbreviated open space in front of the Pantheon was slowly brought to its present state. At some time the eastern end of the porch (to the left as one faces the building, which lies almost exactly north-south) had fallen [9], and this was restored under Urban VIII in the 1620s and Alexander VII in the 1660s; their insignia are visible on the restored capitals and entablature. It was Urban VIII who played the part of another Constans, for he removed some two hundred tons of ancient bronze from the support system of the porch roof. This earned from his affronted subjects, in the best known of all Roman pasquinades, the just coupling of his family name, Barberini, with the barbarian destroyers of the past: *quod non fecerunt barberi fecerunt barberini* (what the barbarians failed to do, the little barbarians did). The metal was chiefly used to cast eighty cannon for Castel Sant'Angelo, Urban saying that it was far better to use it to defend the Holy See than to keep the rain out of the Pantheon porch.

Modern repairs and investigations of the fabric began in the eighteenth century, and though a tasteless stucco décor was applied to the interior attic zone in the 1740s [17], the building has on the whole been properly and respectfully treated since then. The tomb of Victor Emmanuel II [18], the first king of Italy, who died in 1878, was placed in the great west niche (number 13, on illustration 11), that of Umberto I, assassinated in 1900, in the opposite one (number 5). The most recent major restoration and consolidation took place in 1929–34, and at that time the structure of the upper parts of the building was examined in some detail, adding considerably to the understanding of its engineering principles. In more recent years less extensive campaigns of restoration have been carried out. From time

*The model of ancient Rome, portions of which appear in illustrations 15, 19, and 101, is at the Museo della civiltà romana in the E.U.R. suburb of Rome.

Pasquinade

10. The Pantheon; view by Giovannoli, 1616.

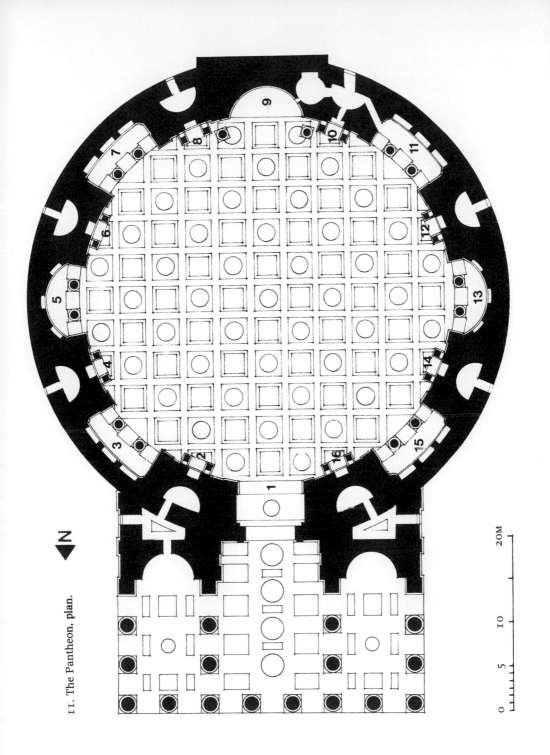

11. The Pantheon, plan.

0　5　10　20M

12. The Pantheon,
intermediate block and the dome.

13. The Pantheon,
dome step-rings.

14 (*below*). The Pantheon
before the removal of the twin towers.

15. Model of the Pantheon area about 300;
some of the details are conjectural.

16. The Pantheon,
with the forecourt restored conjecturally.

to time there have been proposals to alter the rising and constricted space of the Piazza della Rotonda to the north, but understandably enough in a living city nothing has come of these.

Thus the Pantheon, a building dedicated to all the gods and so from its origins conceived as expressing all-inclusive religious meaning and symbolism, has survived intact to a surprising degree. There is enough to study in its tangible state and more than enough in its intangible content. This was well understood by Ammianus Marcellinus, a widely-travelled and intelligent soldier who visited Rome in the suite of the emperor Constantius II, a son of Constantine the Great, in the spring of 357. A stranger to Italy, Constantius toured the celebrated monuments of the city with his officers and the Pantheon was of course on their itinerary. Ammianus' impressions survive in the splendid *History* he later wrote while living in Rome. He found the Pantheon 'like a rounded city region, vaulted over in lofty beauty'. For him, Rome was 'the temple of the whole world'. By his time Rome had already begun to shrink in size, though hardly in reputation. Hadrian's Pantheon stood at its center, the symbol above all others of that lost age when the Mediterranean lands and Europe were united. Surviving, it came gradually also to be a touchstone of architecture in a Christian world, for the universality inherent in its form and meaning was so well and strongly stated that it could stand for all time. Rome was the temple of the whole world, and the Pantheon the temple of all that was Roman. In it, as in few if any other buildings, architecture and continuing history are joined.

17 and 18. The Pantheon:
(*above*) entrance bay from the interior;
(*left*) tomb of Victor Emmanuel II.

19. Model of the Campus Martius as of about 300 ; some of the details are conjectural.

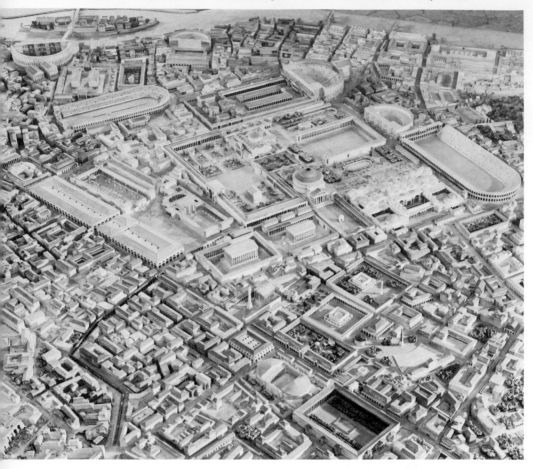

20. Plan of the Pantheon area as of about 300, with the known buildings superimposed upon the modern street plan.

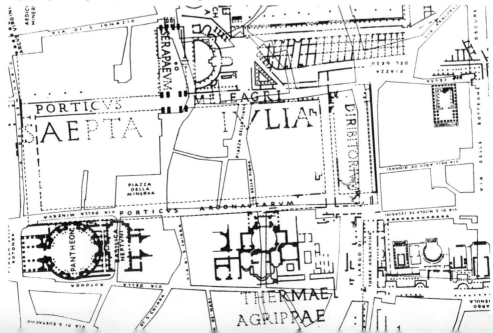

2

THE
BUILDING
PROPER

The Pantheon was placed in axial and right-angled relationships to pre-existing monuments in the central part of the Campus Martius, following the traditional Roman inclination to lay buildings and blocks of buildings out in a more or less rectilinear manner [19 and 20]. Several hundred feet due south of the Pantheon were large public baths built by Agrippa, later restored and enlarged. The west side of the Pantheon forecourt was parallel to the flank of the Baths of Nero, built in the 60s and rebuilt and enlarged in the third century (the model in illustration 15 shows approximations of the later versions of these buildings; see also illustration 20). On the other side of the forecourt and at right angles to its long axis, Hadrian built a temple to his mother-in-law Matidia. To the east of the rotunda proper lay the northern end of the Saepta Julia, an immense walled and porticoed voting precinct begun by Julius Caesar and completed by Agrippa; its central axis was parallel to that of the Pantheon, and it extended to the south for nearly a thousand feet. It ran alongside the east flank of Agrippa's baths; a fragment of the northern part of its niched enclosing wall abuts directly upon the east side of the Pantheon rotunda. All these large structures were in turn enmeshed in a matrix of additional buildings arranged further afield in the same four-square relationships [19].

The paved forecourt of the Pantheon probably extended originally some three or four hundred feet north of the porch, into the vicinity of the church of the Maddalena. The exact details of this court are not known, and those shown here in the model and the restoration drawing [16] are in part conjectural. But there can be no doubt that it was an elongated paved space, surrounded on three sides by covered colonnades or *stoas*. Portions of the paving and some of the column shafts and bases were seen during various excavations; the shafts were of gray granite. At its northern end the court may have been entered through a formal columned gateway or propylon. A triumphal arch stood within the paved area, probably on axis and probably of early second-century date. It carried reliefs showing an emperor as benefactor of the provinces, but its dedication and details are unknown.

Originally there were five marble steps leading up from the pavement level of the court to the floor of the porch, for the Pantheon was set upon a traditional Roman high architectural platform or podium. The rise in the level of the ground around the building, mentioned above, has buried this area to the level of the porch paving [8 and 21]. The porch itself consists of eight unfluted façade columns carrying a triangular stone pediment, the height of which is rather greater, in relation to its width, than was usual in classical temple pediments [2]. Behind this façade there are eight more columns of the same size and design, arranged to form three abbreviated aisles aligned to the south toward the rotunda [11]. All of the outside columns were originally of gray Egyptian granite; the four inside are also of Egyptian granite but of a reddish hue. All have entasis, that is, a subtle diminution of diameter as they rise; all are monoliths; and all have Corinthian capitals and bases of white marble. Of the three aisles, the middle is the widest and leads to the doors of the rotunda. The narrower aisles to the sides terminate in large semi-domed niches where originally statues of Augustus and Agrippa probably stood. All columns carry entablatures, which over the inner two files of columns support piers and arches [22]. This system, together with the exterior columns and their entablatures, once bore the bronze roof structure later removed by Urban VIII. At present, simple wood trusses carry timber framing for the tile covering of the porch. The original bronze structure has often been said also to have been in the form of trusses [cf. 125], but this attributes to ancient bronze a greater structural strength than it may indeed have possessed. Perhaps the bronze was used to sheathe timber trusses of the kind now in place — which may well be those built in the seventeenth century by Urban's carpenters. In any event, the three porch aisles were originally closed overhead by curved ceilings hung from the roof superstructure above [23], that is, imitation barrel vaults of a kind not infrequently used by Roman designers. The pavement, much restored, is of circles, squares, and oblongs of white marble and dark gray granite [11].

The porch is one of the three major and clearly defined parts of the building. The second is the structure containing the niches which, together with the staircase enclosures behind them, rises above the level of the porch roof to form a right-angled intermediate block [12

28

21–3. The Pantheon: detail of the porch;
(*below left*) looking up
into the porch roof structure;
(*below*) upper part of the west side
of the intermediate block, inside the porch.

24 and 25. The Pantheon:
porch roof and intermediate block;
(*right*) rotunda exterior.

26 and 27. The Pantheon: structural diagram;
(*below*) terrace at the foot of the dome,
north side.

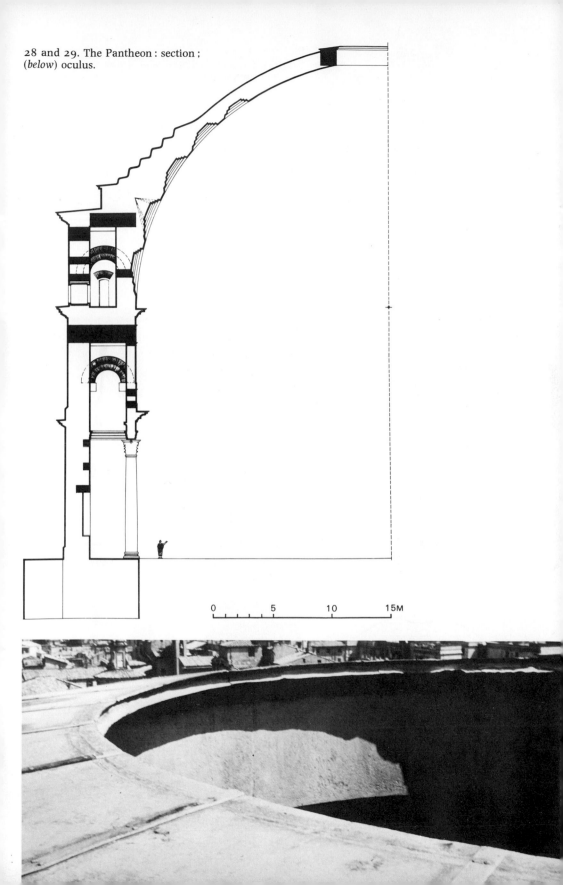

28 and 29. The Pantheon: section;
(*below*) oculus.

30 (*left*). The so-called basilica of Neptune,
abutting the south side of the Pantheon rotunda.

31. The Pantheon, entrance bay vault
and pilaster capitals of the porch.

32. The Pantheon, the doorway.

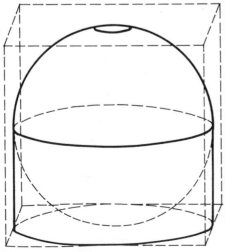

33. The Pantheon,
theoretical spherical and cubical geometry.

34. The Pantheon, light on an aedicula.

and 24]. There are a number of vaulted chambers in its upper stories. The third element is the domed rotunda, almost twice as high as the porch and two-thirds again as wide. On the outside the rotunda reads as an almost solid cylindrical wall of brick [25]. There are openings in it here and there [3], at various levels, that give on to some of the many different chambers that honeycomb the rotunda structure, a honeycombing that is an integral part of a sophisticated engineering solution to the problem of supporting the huge dome [26]. Three cornices encircle the exterior. They are graduated in size from the least projection at the bottom to the greatest at the top. On a level with the top of the intermediate block there is a fairly wide circular terrace, surrounding the dome and sloping downward slightly as it spreads out [27]. Rather more than half of the exterior rise of the dome is defined by a series of concentric step-like rings that are actually buttresses [13], masses of masonry placed over the dome's lower part where they are most needed structurally (they also facilitated construction, as will be seen). By providing greater weight downward, they help to counteract the tendency of the dome to push outward. In other words, if the dome were thinner in this area, it would rupture and collapse. In engineering this is known as a compression system: the building is stabilized by superposed weight properly placed.

Partly because of these ring buttresses, the exterior silhouette of the dome is not hemispherical but bowl-shaped; inside, the hemispherical surface of the dome rises from a level well below that of the outer high terrace. The upper part of the cylindrical wall of the rotunda is built up high, also as a shoulder-like buttress, reducing the prominence of the exterior of the dome [28]. The only exterior spherical portion rises above the highest of the step-ring buttresses, extending upward and inward to culminate in a horizontal circular opening, an oculus, thirty feet in diameter, that is centered over the paving a hundred and fifty feet below [29].

The intermediate block, the rotunda, and the dome are made almost entirely of concrete. The bricks of the cylinder are a mere skin over the concrete structure, and the dome is of poured concrete. There are, here and there in the fabric, structural elements of stone, and there are powerful thick vaults of tile-shaped bricks radiating out through the rotunda cylinder over the big interior niches at ground level and the enclosed chambers above [26]. These vaults help carry the load of the superstructure downward, distributing it on to what are, in effect, eight great piers. These piers appear on the plan [11], between the niches, as U-shaped masses turned outwards (even-numbered positions). The outer ends of the radiating tile vaults can be seen on the rotunda exterior [3 and 25].

33

At the south of the rotunda and abutting on it are the remains of a great hall, transverse to the main axis of the Pantheon and about as wide as the rotunda [15, 20, and 30]. This may be the Basilica of Neptune, first built by Agrippa and restored or rebuilt by Hadrian. Although in many plans and photographs it appears to be a part of the Pantheon, it was not accessible in antiquity from the interior of the rotunda and is not part of our subject.

The interior of the rotunda can be gained only by way of the porch and through the bronze doors. The space or bay just outside the doors is still covered by its original recessed (coffered) barrel vault [31], and round about are inscriptions of various dates that commemorate events connected with the building's long history. On the walls are some handsome Hadrianic marble reliefs, but not all are in their original positions. The workmanship and detailing of the Corinthian pilasters of the entrance bay, also of white marble, are of great grace of execution, rather Augustan in spirit and quality. The white marble of these orders, though darkened by time and battered here and there, still plays off effectively against the tinted but sombre unfluted granite columns of the porch proper. Bronze pilasters frame the doors, which are of bronze sheets nailed to massive wooden frames; they were restored in the time of Pius IV (1559–65). Around the whole is a much admired, and copied, marble enframement of classical inspiration [32]. Within this frame, above the doors, there is a bronze grille which, because of the deep hood of the porch, admits little light into the interior. Beyond the doors there is a vaulted bay corresponding in depth to the thickness of the rotunda cylinder; beyond that, only the unencumbered expanse of Hadrian's masterpiece.

The controlling geometry of the interior surfaces of the rotunda is generated from a vertical center line, an invisible axis that rises from the middle of the paving and passes up through the center of the oculus above. In any given horizontal plane, all distances outward from this vertical line to the cylindrical wall or the hemispherical dome are of course equal, being radii. The Pantheon is the example *par excellence* of this kind of design, known in the history of architecture as a centralized building. In such a building the major controlling axis, the central line from which the symmetry of the building is evolved, is vertical, rather than horizontal, as it is in, say, a Christian basilica, where the space takes the form of an oblong box with entrance and altar opposite each other at the shorter ends. In the interior of the Pantheon, the vertical cylinder and the hemispherical dome are of equal height, and the radius and height of the cylinder are the same [33]. The curving wall of the cylinder is marked off into two horizontal

34

zones of unequal height by a large cornice that runs round the interior. This drops back into the entrance bay and along the base of the concave vault of the open niche or apse opposite, for these two features break boldly up into the second zone [81]. That zone in turn is capped by a second large cornice that girdles the entire interior at the base of the great dome.

The implicit pure geometry of these curving surfaces is broken up by design features large and small. In the first zone, from the floor level to the cornice, there are eight very large recesses whose spaces draw back from the cylinder wall (the odd-numbered positions of illustration 11). The entrance bay and the apse form two of these. The other six are symmetrically and radially disposed right and left, each screened by two marble columns. The transverse or east-west niches (numbers 5 and 13 of illustration 11) have rear walls more curved in plan than those on the diagonal axes. Between these huge niches there project from the cylinder wall, in front of the hidden piers, eight temple-fronts or aediculae (sometimes called tabernacles; the even-numbered positions of illustration 11). These are raised on high podia and were originally alike — they have been altered a good deal — except that the four closest to the transverse axis have curved (segmental) pediments, while the other four carry triangular ones of a traditional kind [Title page and 34]. The result is a scenic, theatre-like wall [82], richly worked with light and shade, cornerless and continuous.

aedicula

The floor is paved in squares, and circles in squares, of colored granites, marbles, and porphyry [11 and 35]. The grid of this is aligned with the main north-south direction of the building and its surface rises slightly toward the center. It was re-laid in 1873 but the effect is genuinely Hadrianic. The circles and squares are so related that continuous files of either appear only along diagonal lines; that is, the circles are arranged like checkers on a board set up for play. There is a circle at the center of the whole, and as a result there are alternating lines of circles and squares along the main and transverse axes, and lines of circles connecting the diagonal niches, 3 with 11, and 7 with 15. Thus the paving, in color, texture, and design, is an inseparable artistic part of the whole tinted envelope of space.

Floor

1873

The colors of the floor are repeated and augmented in the architecture and sheathing of the first zone roundabout. The columns that screen the diagonal niches (3, 7, 11, and 15) and their flanking pilasters are of yellowish-orange marble, giallo antico — ancient yellow — from Numidia (western Tunisia and eastern Algeria). The other two niches, 5 and 13, and the forward-standing columns beside the apse, 9, are of a multi-colored marble, chiefly off-white with large red and

1 zone

35

35. The Pantheon, pavement and west wall.

reddish-purple markings, pavonazzetto – peacock marble – quarried in central Asia Minor (Turkey). Deep red-purple Egyptian porphyry was used in the orders of some of the projecting aediculae, as well as in the encircling cornices that limit the horizontal zones. The pier and niche surfaces, as well as the wall of the second or attic zone, were originally sheathed in marble, with many circle-and-square patterns. As in the aediculae, much has been lost, and there are many places where plaster, painted to imitate colored marbles, has replaced the original stones. From the fair amount of original sheathing that remains, it is clear that white, green, and green-gray augmented the colors mentioned above. Except for the trabeation (columns, entablatures and pediments), these marbles of the two cylindrical zones were only veneer, thin sheets sawn from blocks, shaped to the approximate outline of the pattern required and then, after dressing, fixed to the brick-faced concrete with bronze clamps ingeniously slotted into the unseen flush edges of the sheets.

In the ancient design of the second zone, a high band of blue-white marble lay beneath a repeating pattern of pilasters and blind windows. A veneering of circles and rectangles filled in the areas between the porphyry pilasters and over the windows. The latter, which alternately give on to the vaulted spaces over the niches, were presumably fitted originally with gilded bronze grilles. A section of the eighteenth-century stucco work has been removed from this second zone at positions 11 and 12 and replaced with a reproduction of a portion of the original system [36].

36. The Pantheon, restored attic zone and environs.

37

In the third interior zone, that of the dome, the visual events con-
continue in a great swirl around the whole circle [37]. The surface is
that of a hemisphere, apparently resting upon the second belt cornice;
only apparently, because the lower part of what is seen is actually the
inner surface of the superposed, rising wall-buttress system mentioned
above, and the interior cornice is at almost the same level as the second
or middle exterior one [28]. Thus, the upper interior cornice defines
the impost plane, or springing level, of the dome as it is perceived
from the interior. Above it, the first of the five rows of geometrically
shaped coffers begins. These are quite complicated shapes, not only
because they are formed from surfaces of double curvature*, but also
because they are designed upon perspective principles. Their enboxed
sides recede slanting inward, as if each frame-like element of each
coffer was the base portion or frustum of an oblique pyramid whose
apex lay outside and above the dome [38, and cf 96]. There are one
hundred and forty coffers; as they rise, they diminish in size and
depth, and they leave between them a strongly marked grid of rib-like
appearance. Almost certainly, each coffer was edged with moldings
similar to those surviving in the coffering near the so-called Hippodrome on the Palatine [39], and each carried a large gilded bronze
rosette at its center, anchored in the concrete. At the very top of the
dome, the nearly horizontal surface closes to the ring of the oculus.
There was once a gilded bronze moulding of classical design around
this ring; only a part of it remains [Frontispiece and 98].

About nine-tenths of the structure of the intermediate block and the
rotunda is of concrete. An amorphous material, concrete takes the
shape given it by temporary forms of wood or, in the case of much
Roman imperial wall and pier construction, of relatively thin shells of
brick which, upon the drying of the whole mass, become inextricably
bonded into it. The Pantheon rotunda walls were built by pouring
concrete into low, wide trenches formed by the inner and outer brick
walls, the trenches rising precisely one upon another until the dome
terrace level was reached. The dome was poured over an immense
hemispherical wooden form, supported by a forest of timbers and
struts, upon which the negative wooden molds for the coffers were
fixed.

Between manufacture and setting hard in structure, concrete is
formless and so to speak in limbo, ready to obey architectural instruction. It is an agent for casting, and this suggests curved and

*A surface of single curvature is one on which a straight line can be drawn,
for example a tin can; this cannot be done on one of double curvature, such as a
beach ball or a pear.

38

37. The Pantheon, the dome.

38. The Pantheon, detail of coffering.

39. The Palatine, Rome, detail of coffering to the south-east of the so-called Hippodrome.

40. Making tile arches over wooden formwork, Kuşadası, Turkey.

41. Making tile arches over wooden formwork.

rather complex shapes, provided the carpenters who make the necessary temporary forms can do the job. The labor requirements, the technology, and the processes are different from those employed when buildings are made from stone precisely cut and fitted. This is not to say that the Pantheon could not have been made from cut stone – probably it could have been, witness the great stone domed nineteenth-century church of St Mary at Mosta on the island of Malta, not all that much smaller than the Pantheon [150 and 151]. But poured concrete was a more suitable structural material for the building envisaged by Hadrian and his architect, a monumental interior space vaulted over. This was partly because of the kind of disciplined manpower available, more or less regimented gangs of unskilled and semi-skilled labor who could be used effectively in this kind of construction, where the actual physical work consisted mostly of mixing, hauling, carrying, and pouring, rather than dressing blocks of stone to exact dimensions. In the construction of the Pantheon several very highly skilled specialists were necessary – the architect, of course, the master carpenters, and the master masons who directed the bricklaying [40 and 41] – but the skilled craftsmen needed for the construction of a classical temple in marble were not required except for the portico and the interior orders. By using structural materials that were in themselves insignificant and anonymous – lime, sand, and bricks – the organization of workmen and their relationship to the flow of materials and the timing of pouring concrete was brought into line with the Roman predilection for clearly defined and efficient organization.

So the Pantheon was built on an immense deep ring foundation of concrete. As the dome was poured upon its temporary wooden hemisphere, its outer surfaces were determined at first by the circular brick dams that formed the step-ring buttresses [27]. Above the uppermost step-ring, the more nearly horizontal fabric of the dome would have been fashioned from tacky concrete, reaching finally to the horizontal rings of tiles, set vertically, that ingeniously closed the fabric around the void of the oculus. Armies of workmen, scheduled according to the drying time of the mortar, swarmed along the exterior scaffolding, and up and down the ladders and ramps, while others operated the multi-pulleyed cranes and did the scores of jobs attendant upon the construction of a great building. As the concrete dried, the marble fitters, bronze workers, and other specialists occupied the inner woodwork, finishing and decorating the interior surfaces.

Roman order, one observes; the Roman passion for sequence and organization, for carefully thinking out interrelationships between one

42

thing and another, necessary of course to the success of all major construction, but followed through by the Romans with great thoroughness. An example will perhaps suffice. All concrete has in it broken rock or other fragmented material called aggregate. This is heavier, when the structure has dried out and cured, than its surrounding mortar matrix of chemically allied lime and sand. It increases the mass of the concrete and makes it stronger, able to support more weight than mortar could without it. But high up in a concrete structure the need to support weight is of course much less than it is in foundations and supporting walls below. In the Pantheon the weight of the kinds of aggregate used decreases regularly in layered, clearly differentiated zones as the height of the building increases. The heaviest appears in the foundations, the next lightest in the lower walls, and so on to the upper part of the dome, where pumice, which is very porous and light, was used. Some time about 125–8 the last of the vast temporary wood structure was removed. Modern engineering calculations show that the Roman engineers' methods were correct. They must have been, as the building still stands, and the five thousand-odd tons of concrete that form the dome are still in place.

No single moment in this building process was as dramatic as that in high medieval construction when the soaring nave vault of a Gothic cathedral was decentered — when the supporting woodwork was lowered slightly to reveal a marvelously thin shell of stone, arching up and across a void fifty or more feet wide, standing free and clear. And the Pantheon does not have the luminous and moving sculptural presence of a major Greek temple of the fifth century B.C. But that is as it should be. The architect was not trying to do what others had done or would do. He was, at Hadrian's orders, seeking something ineluctably Roman, something in architecture that spoke of the new and many-sided culture of later antiquity, of that phase of world-experience called the Roman Empire. But before examining this aspect of the Pantheon, it will perhaps be useful to observe the building more purely as a work of architecture, both in relationship to earlier buildings and as the result of the process of architectural design.

3

BACKGROUND
AND
PRINCIPLES OF DESIGN

Round buildings were fairly common in antiquity before the Pantheon. A circular exterior allows the greatest enclosed area a given length of wall can provide, and a plain circular building is easy to lay out. A stake with a line looped around it for the radius is, essentially, all that is needed, and this in comparatively primitive times was often easier to manage than the establishment of right angles properly related. But sophisticated cylindrical buildings pose problems. They have by themselves no axis on the ground, so that the suitable identification of an entrance, its effective architectural expression or articulation, is not always easy. It is as difficult to relate curving walls to a projecting entranceway as it is to relate them to urban surroundings. A circular form needs either a good deal of open space around it, so that it can stand free, or else it needs to be embedded in other structures, as in a Syrian beehive village, or a town of round houses or trulli in Apulia – or a Roman bath building [101]. Half-way measures with the exterior settings of round buildings are usually visually unsatisfactory, while if a round structure is large the problem of roofing it becomes rather formidable. Because of such things, most pre-Pantheon circular buildings were not of monumental scale and most were not conceived as enclosing usable interior volumes. In many cases, ancient round structures were not intended to be entered at all, or were entered only by a few persons, such as the priestly celebrants of a religious cult, or a magnate's family gathered for a funeral ceremony in a round tomb. The monumental public building of round plan, vaulted over and emphatically intended to be entered, was a creation of Roman imperial architects.

The idea of circularity in monumental architecture descended chiefly from two sources, religious buildings and tombs; though circular huts existed in Greco-Roman times, circular houses did not.

Each type of building had a very ancient ancestry indeed, and each type appeared in both exterior and interior versions. That is, there are examples both of tombs and temples that were conceived as enclosures for interior volumes, and of those where only the exterior design counted and the interior, if any, was minimal and accessible to very few persons. An early and famous example of a volumetric tomb is the so-called Treasury of Atreus, dating from about 1300 B.C., at Mycenae in southern Greece [42]. This magnificent structure, sunken into a hillside, was approached by a long paved walk or dromos at the bottom of a man-made trough or miniature canyon. The circular interior, somewhat less than a third of the diameter of the Pantheon, was covered by a vault-like shape made of stones carefully laid horizontally in circles, whose diameters decrease in such a way as to form a surface rather like that of the more pointed end of an egg.

The opposite, or negative, of this kind of interiorized tomb was the tumulus, a rounded burial mound of earth, frequently of great size, common around the eastern Mediterranean and in some places in the west as well. A tumulus often indicates the burial place of royalty. In Hellenistic or later Greek times (about 300–50 B.C.), as well as in the Roman world, these were sometimes grand constructions built up partly of stone. In any case, tumuli are all but solid, containing a corridor or two and a burial chamber. There are scores of Etruscan examples. During the Roman republic (the last few centuries B.C.) and the empire (begun in 27 B.C.), many smaller [43] and architecturally quite elaborate [44] circular tombs also appeared. These and similar structures were sometimes small versions of round temples, either open or solid, usually mounted on square bases; examples of this type descend in a general way from the celebrated monument to Lysicrates in Athens, of the late fourth century B.C. [45]. Both Augustus and Hadrian built huge, circular, semi-solid tombs of concrete for themselves; both are in Rome [46 and 47]. The tradition of roundness was very strongly entrenched in funerary architecture.

For our purposes, the other line, that of religious buildings, is probably more significant. Those that were meant to be seen only from the exterior were fairly common, and both the Greeks and Romans built them; they are called tholoi, in the singular tholos. In Greece there were famous examples at such central shrines as Delphi and Epidauros [48]. From Greek models, the Romans derived such examples as the round temple by the Tiber in Rome, a so-called Temple of Vesta [49], and the magnificently sited version at Tivoli [50]. In all such buildings, Greek or Roman, the fairly small central cylindrical structure or cella is surrounded by a ring of columns, and it is this

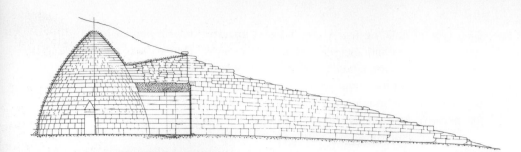

42 (*top*). Mycenae, the so-called
Treasury of Atreus, fourteenth century B.C.

43 (*above left*). Tiddis, Algeria,
tomb of the Lollii, second century.

44 (*above right*). Le Médracen, Algeria,
late second century B.C.

45 (*right*). Athens, monument to Lysicrates,
late fourth century B.C.

46 (*opposite above*). The Mausoleum
of Augustus, Rome, 28 B.C.

47 (*opposite below*). The Mausoleum
of Hadrian, Rome (Castel S. Angelo),
late 130s.

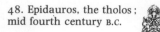

48. Epidauros, the tholos;
mid fourth century B.C.

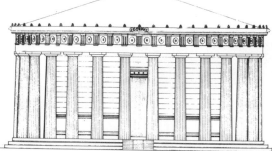

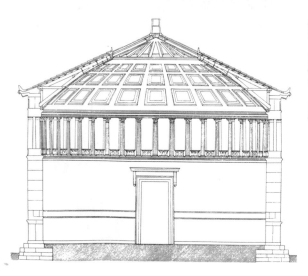

49 (*top*). The so-called Temple of Vesta
(detail), Rome, early first century B.C.

50 (*above*). The so-called Temple
of Vesta, Tivoli, early first century B.C.,
view by Piranesi, 1756.

51 (*left*). The Arsinoeion, Samothrace,
Greece, section restored.

ring, together with its base and superstructure, that makes up the architecture of the building. The cella had a door, and inside it was a space roofed by a conical timber frame supporting the roof tiles, but this interior space was not normally open to the public, being used only to house cult objects and perhaps now and then for some ceremony. As so often in official ancient religion, the cult building was an architectural backdrop for ceremonies that took place outdoors.

With the volumetric or interiorized cult building, we are of course closer to the conception that lay behind the Pantheon rotunda. It seems to have been in Hellenistic times that such buildings appeared, buildings round and fairly plain on their exteriors, without colonnades. They were usually free-standing, and almost always were dedicated to a non-official, that is non-Olympian, god, goddess, or group of deities. The largest in the Greek world stood on the island of Samothrace in the northern part of the Aegean. Though the exterior was quite richly articulated, it was the uncolumned shell of an interior hall [51]. Some sixty feet in diameter, it was dedicated to the Great Gods by Queen Arsinoë II some time in the 280s B.C. There are a number of examples of this kind of round building with sizeable interior spaces, and their use has much to do with the rapid growth of mystery cults around the eastern Mediterranean, cults requiring secret initiation and instruction. The remains of one such building have been found as far away as Old Nisa on the river Oxus, east of the Caspian Sea, in what is now the Turkmenistan S.S.R. It seems to be of Greco-Parthian inspiration, and of late Hellenistic or imperial date; the interior diameter is also about sixty feet. In the Latin west, however, it was chiefly the columned round temple or tholos that flourished. Mystery cults caught on in the west later than in the east, and when they did the Roman government tried from time to time to suppress them. By the time they had gained permanent footholds, Roman architecture was shifting strongly toward new kinds of interior spaces, and the two developments met and mingled.

But this is by no means the whole story. The building technology based on cast concrete, described above, began to become effective in Italy from the third century B.C., at first quite slowly and then with rapidly increasing momentum. By the first century it had been perfected, if not entirely accepted. It is chiefly along this avenue that circularity in architecture spread to a number of other building types, most importantly, from the point of view of exploring the ancestry of the Pantheon, to baths (thermae) and palaces and villas. Other kinds of structures, solid and hollow, must also be recalled in tracing the skein of influences and combinations involved; for example, centralized

49

designs other than tombs or cult buildings, such as hexagonal and round towers. But it is bath structures and palaces, and to a lesser degree market buildings, that figure most importantly in the story during the century and a half of imperial rule and consolidation that preceded Hadrian's accession.

There is a fairly large number of relevant buildings and fragments of buildings from that period. Only three will be considered here in any detail, and perhaps they can stand for all. The first is a domed rotunda of a bath complex, probably of Augustan date, that still stands at Baia on the north shore of the Bay of Naples [52]. This structure, known traditionally as a Temple of Mercury, is about half the diameter of the Pantheon and about one-eighth the volume, assuming its height is equal to its diameter. Because it is partly filled with water, its exact vertical dimensions are not known. It stands shouldered into a steep hillside, and originally it was surrounded by other elements of the bath complex. It therefore required no external entrance, and its two internal openings were reached through a corridor and a flanking salon respectively. The internal shape is simply that of a cylinder carrying a hemisphere, with four niches placed diagonally, two windows in the lower slope of the dome, and an oculus [53]. The structure that supports the dome is made of a rough concrete of smallish stones and ample mortar, a kind of powerful rubble finished off at the surface with patterned stonework. The dome is of a similar kind of concrete, with the stones placed more or less radially to the dome's curve, rather in the manner of the wedge-shaped radiating elements of a stone arch (voussoirs), but without any surface finish and set in an enveloping and shaping mass of mortar, the whole laid and poured over wooden formwork [54]. The interior surfaces and space, and the effect of the lighting through the oculus, are similar to those of the Pantheon, though the surfaces are less articulated and the scale is more human and comprehensible. Here, at a seaside pleasure resort, an Augustan architect could design in a mode that would probably have been unacceptable in Rome for an official building of the period. In Pompeii, across the Bay, there are smaller examples of domed round rooms, in bath buildings, that are lit by oculi, and this kind of shape is common in thermal architecture throughout the empire. The genealogy of this form can be traced to simpler Greek baths that incorporated small round rooms, sometimes cut from living rock beside their spring or other source of water.

Between Baia and Naples, at Pozzuoli, there is a market-place composed of a large rectangle bordered by shops and shrines. In the center stood a sort of tholos [55], a circle of sixteen marble columns

52 and 53. The so-called
Temple of Mercury, Baia:
view from above,
and (*right*) interior.

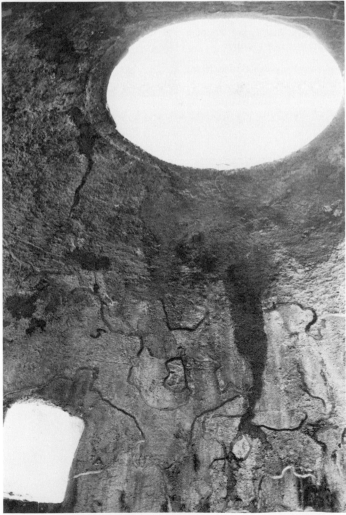

54 (*top*). The so-called
Temple of Mercury, Baia,
section of dome,
seen during restoration.

55 (*right*). The Market, Pozzuoli,
begun late first century.

56. Nero's Golden House, Rome,
mid-first century;
model of the octagonal atrium.

57 and 58. Nero's Golden House, Rome:
(*right*) dome of the octagonal atrium
(detail), and plan of the octagonal atrium.

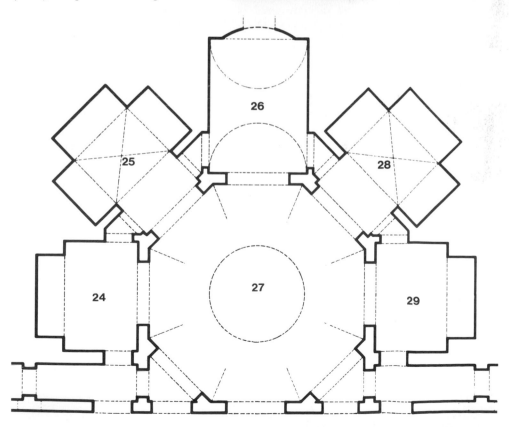

on a platform reached by four flights of steps on the cardinal axes. In the center there was a fountain; the ring of columns may have been surmounted by a conical roof. There was no cella and one looked through the screen of columns to the fountain and beyond. As with the circular bath form, the centralized market structure, usually set in a shopping plaza, was common in the Roman world. Circular buildings could serve many functions.

Our second major example stands in Rome, the octagonal atrium of a very large wing of Nero's palace of the later 60s known as the Golden House. Though shorn of its mosaics, marbles, and gilding, with its waterworks silenced, the bare structure of this exceptional design says more about the revolution in architecture that accompanied the establishment of the imperial system than any other first-century building we have [56]. It is relevant here because it was not a cult, funeral, or bath building, but a palace hall for a ruler who claimed to be cosmocrator; because it was built in a concrete technology fully mastered; and most of all because it is a centralized structure with toed-in subordinate spaces round about, chiefly lit by an oculus. Its structural scheme, though complex and sophisticated, is only the servant of a radically new, and very exciting, approach to space-making. The Golden House octagon is clearly the direct ancestor of an immense number of centralized buildings. That it is of octagonal rather than circular plan is no bar to its relationship to the Pantheon; here perhaps one may invoke Krautheimer's dictum, originally direc-ted at medieval church architecture, that all buildings with more than four sides are round. In other words, the Neronian octagon is in every sense a centralized space.

At this point in time, the claims of the imperial system, the perfec-tion of concrete construction, and the Romans' urge to express in interior spaces their architectural talents all coalesced. Nero's octag-onal atrium is the epitome of this process, its creation hastened by the opportunities to build and the lessons about flammable materials provided by a great fire that levelled a quarter or more of Rome in the summer of 64. And the emperor, at twenty-six, loved novelty and re-jected tradition as much as he dared. Severus, his architect, and Celer, his master builder, were certainly not traditional men. They created a work of art that represents the first culminating stage in the creation of centralized interior architecture. The second is the Pantheon, the third a building called the Temple of Minerva Medica (which we will meet in a later chapter), and then come such major works as S. Costanza, S. Vitale, and SS. Serigus and Bacchus; the select list con-continues to the present. Surely, as Ward-Perkins says of Nero's octagon 'it is hardly an exaggeration to say that the whole subsequent history of European architectural thought hangs upon this historic event.'

What Severus and Celer created was a cage-like structure composed of eight piers set at the angles of an octagon, surrounding and composing, with an umbrella-like vault overhead, an airy and well-lit space [57 and 58]. One side of this octagon was a part of the long façade of the wing, and the two adjoining sides give on to connecting transverse corridors parallel to the façade. The other five sides open between the piers onto rooms of different shapes, the two transverse ones being in effect very deep niches covered with barrel vaults and ending in smaller vaulted niches of the same vertical outline as their main spaces. The two on the diagonals (numbers 25 and 28 on the plan, illustration 58) are cross-shaped and so vaulted, and the axial one, deeper than the rest, is rectangular in plan and barrel vaulted; in this last a display of water flowed down a sloping channel. The central vault rises from a level just above the eight openings between the piers, and it modulates gradually from an octagon to a seamless dome of nearly spherical surface, culminating in a proportionately broad oculus. Over its outer sloping sides, light was admitted under inclined vaults to the five radiating chambers. The whole was of concrete, brick-faced below the springing lines of the vaults, and poured on to forms above. The whole unit is embedded in the palace wing proper, thus there is no exterior or periphery. The entire concept was generated from and is composed around an all-important but invisible vertical center line. No columns rise from the pavement level, and the openings into the radially disposed rooms are unscreened, but the disposition and nature of the shapes of those rooms are clearly in the manner of the Pantheon design. There are no unnecessary solids, for the arrangement of the elements of the composition is clever and economical. Shape, space, structure, and light are interlocked as one; in the words of another age, nothing needs to be added or taken away. The fact that the building is a centralized one in great part makes these qualities possible. The potential for varied space-making in this kind of design intrigued the architects of later antiquity, and from it they wrought a number of superb buildings.

First, then, one might say, came engineering – bridges, aqueducts and warehouses – that took ever greater advantage of concrete. Lessons from the Greek world, especially from the architecture of its later, Hellenistic phase, were not lost upon the Roman architects. Interiorized architecture, changes in building methods, and the creation of a monarchy whose ecumenical claims were suitably symbolized by the round building, all played parts in the story. By

59. The Markets of Trajan, Rome, interior of a semi-domed hall, c. 105–10.

60 (*below*). The cross-vault principle.

61 (*bottom*). The Markets of Trajan, Rome, great hall, analytical perspective.

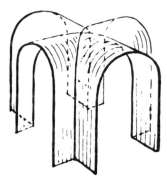

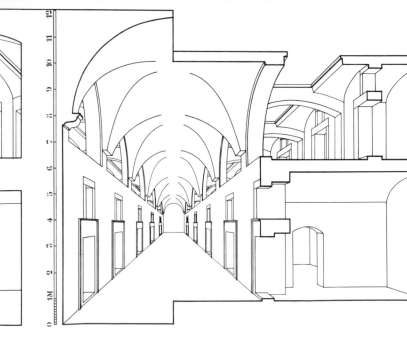

the end of the first century A.D., the domed centralized hall, though not yet a commonplace in the Roman world, was a building type known and well understood. Our third example, the Markets of Trajan in Rome, of about 105–10, has no domed centralized spaces but is important for other reasons. The Markets show that vaulted, brick-faced architecture had become fully accepted and could be used in almost any kind of building. Since they were built just a few years before the Pantheon, they clearly record the kind of design and construction that Hadrian's architects knew well and perhaps even worked on. And in spite of the obvious differences in form and use between the Markets and the Pantheon, there are important similarities.

One, which is probably self-evident from the illustrations and the discussion above of the Pantheon's structure, is that they were built with the same structural technique [59]. Secondly, both are the products of a desire to express and define the new architecture in a monumental way. The Markets were very large. Some one hundred and seventy rooms, including several large vaulted halls, still exist; the original extent of the complex is unknown. Trajan's builders developed ideas here which, though they had been tentatively put forward before, had never had such play. Scores of vaulted shops (tabernae) were built to standard sizes. The cross vault [60], the product of the right-angled intersection of two barrel vaults, was repeated along a common axis and used to cover a large longitudinal space. The earlier history of the cross vault is rather obscure. In the octagonal atrium of the Golden House it had been used on a small scale in the two chambers on the diagonals [58], and it may have achieved monumental size in the lost baths built in Rome for the emperor Titus (79–81). In the 80s, it was used over some of the curving corridors of the Colosseum. Whatever the story of its evolution may properly be, Trajan's architect used it in what at present reading appears to be a new setting.

In the upper reaches of the Markets, there is a large space, fashioned like a covered street, that foreshadows the Pantheon to a considerable degree [61]. Overhead are the repeated cross vaults, whose side arches give light and air to the whole [62]. These arches also define the edges of two longitudinal galleries [63], and all around, at right angles to the main long axis of the composition, are vaulted tabernae [64]. That is, as in the Neronian octagon and the Pantheon, there is a central main vaulted space with surrounding vaulted elements placed in symmetrical subordination both functionally and structurally. The architect exploited with great finesse the fact that it is possible to construct cross vaults so that they are supported only at their corners.

57

By connecting a series of these vaults in line, he gained a barrel-vaulted space without the massive solids a barrel vault requires and the dim lighting it causes. Instead of continuous vault surfaces above the supporting walls, the Markets hall has arcades formed by the reiterated, open ends of the cross vaults. Light and air are admitted freely into the central space in a wonderfully effective design; whoever invented the multi-bayed, cross-vaulted hall was a very great architect. The Markets hall is a rectilinear forerunner of the Pantheon: both have an ingenious relationship between structure and counter-structure bottom to top, both use symmetrically subordinate spaces without their appearing tacked on or anonymous in terms of visual and spatial composition, and both have monumentality of scale. If by some metamorphosis the Markets hall could be made circular, without altering the conceptual relationships of its elements, a Pantheon-like building would result, for the same kind of thinking produced both buildings.

There are also in the Markets of Trajan some semi-circular vaulted spaces. It may suffice to point out that these halls, closed along a diameter of their arc by a straight wall, are semi-domed, with compression systems, in at least one case, of more or less step-ring form [65]. In the largest of these spaces, the straight wall is articulated by niches alternately round-headed and flat [59]. Everywhere in the Markets, the architect's excitement at the possibilities of vaulting is apparent — in lighting, in new shapes for spaces, and in relationships between solids and voids. The revolutionary, non-Greek architecture of the Roman empire had come to stay and, in this extraordinary example of Roman social architecture, the old design vocabulary of the past, the classical orders, is conspicuously absent.

In Hadrianic times, the architectural strains of the past, distant and immediate as well, were brought together in creative synthesis. The vaulted style had been combined with the orders before, but never with such harmony nor on such a scale. At his huge, sprawling villa at Tivoli near Rome — more like a private and personal town than a traditional villa — Hadrian experimented with architectural design to his heart's content. At the villa there was a sort of Pantheon, the Temple of Apollo [66 and 67], and an intricate circular composition of the Pantheon's exact diameter and of the same date [68]. This, the Maritime Theatre, was not vaulted over, but consisted of a circular gallery around a moat around an island, a centralized scheme indeed. Not far away are a number of other column-with-vault buildings, some of great originality and grace, such as the elaborate nymphaeum or fountain house at the end of the plaza of waterworks known as the

62–5. The Markets of Trajan,
Rome :
(*right*) great hall, vaulting ;
(*below*) great hall, gallery ;
(*bottom left*) great hall ;
(*bottom right*) vault construction.

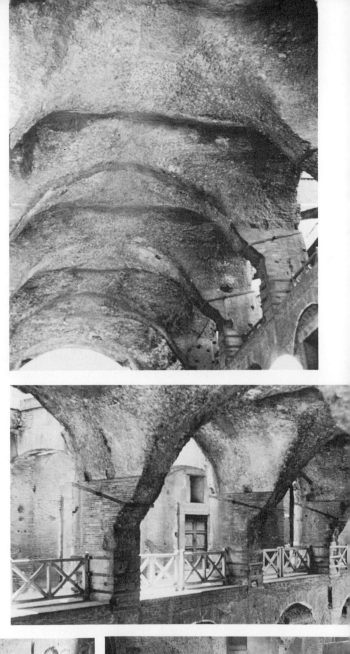

Piazza d'Oro. And beside one long pool stood a row of Greek caryatids*. The point is that by Hadrian's time, the grand traditions of classical architecture — by his day, over five centuries old — were married to the more youthful vaulted style, a marriage of dynastic styles of the highest rank, one with profound implications for all subsequent Mediterranean and European architecture.

The stylistic distance between the architecture of Hadrian's time and that of the beginning of the empire can be measured by considering what is known of Agrippa's original Pantheon of 25 B.C. and comparing it with Hadrian's. The written sources tell us only about certain of the statues in and on Agrippa's building, and that the sculpture was, at least in part, from the hand of an Athenian artist named Diogenes; works by others were added later. Two specific groups of statuary were made by Diogenes: an unspecified number of caryatids and a composition of figures, not identified, set in the lofty fastigium or pediment. Pliny the Elder (23–79) says that the caryatids [cf. 95] were very well done, but that the fastigium group, though equally good, was not so well known because it was so high up. Thus the original building, like so much official art of the Augustan age, was very much in the Greek manner. The chief sculptor was Greek and the building featured caryatids, popular and famous in ancient Greece, not only because of their presence on the Erechtheion on the Athenian acropolis, but also from other examples in Greece and Asia Minor. The building had a traditional, sculptured fastigium, and although this fact alone does not preclude the presence of a vaulted cella, our knowledge of the principles of official Augustan architecture in Rome does: it was all trabeated.

In the late 1890s, excavations were made in and beside the Pantheon to try, among other things, to learn more about Agrippa's building. For a variety of reasons the results, as published, were rather inconclusive, but it appears probable that the Agrippan building was a rectangular one, set where the Pantheon porch is now, but facing the other way, that is, to the south. In general lines it seems to have followed Greek precedent, whereby sanctuaries dedicated to all the gods were fairly simple rectilinear precincts. The long axis of the building was east-west, at right angles to that of its porch, which projected south from the main body of the building and presumably carried the fastigium to which Pliny refers; pedimented porches had appeared on the long sides of cult buildings before. It was not, therefore, in the form of a classical temple, Greek or Roman. This information,

*Draped female figures functioning as columns.

66. Hadrian's Villa near Tivoli, *c.* 123, model showing the Temple of Apollo, upper right.

67 and 68. Hadrian's Villa
near Tivoli:
ruins of the Temple of Apollo,
view by Piranesi, 1756;
(*right*) air view of the remains of the
Maritime Theatre and surroundings.

sketchy though it is, can in good conscience be combined with Pliny's remarks to evoke the image of a rectangular, lofty, trabeated building with classical sculptural décor of high quality, the whole covered with wood-framed roofs over the main space and the projecting porch. Attempts have been made to reconstruct the plan and elevation on paper and to locate the caryatids, but the data are really insufficient for this. Enough is known, however, to say with certainty that Hadrian's Pantheon was of another kind of architecture altogether, in spite of the apparently traditional design of its forecourt and porch.

The forecourt seems to have been about as wide as the rotunda and somewhat more than twice as long [15 and 16]. From the point of view of the exterior design of the building, the most important fact to recognize about the forecourt is that it was so much lower than the present paving level. Because of this, and because of the length of the court, the appearance of the Pantheon in antiquity would have been different from what it is today. As the court was traversed to the south, the exterior of the dome would gradually have sunk down behind the intermediate block and porch, and the stoa colonnades would in part have obscured the rounded sides of the cylinder beyond. The whole forecourt composition formed, in path and perspective, a visual frame for the Pantheon proper. This was all the more effective because the elements of the colonnades were on a small scale, in contrast to those of the porch beyond, which loomed enormous at the end of the flat expanse of paving. From the central area of the court, the porch filled one's vision, in the manner of a traditional temple standing at the foot of the open ceremonial space before it. This ancient relationship of clearing and temple had by imperial times become fixed on an axial system, as in the templed fora of the emperors, so that the Pantheon forecourt and porch were composed in a familiar and particularly Roman way.

The porch pavement was gained by a flight of five steep steps almost as wide as the porch, itself somewhat wider than the Athenian Parthenon. As so often in Roman monumental architecture, the major dimensions are in units or multiples of five Roman feet*. Thus the porch is 115 Roman feet wide, the great monolithic columns five feet in diameter, the oculus 30. This does not however mean that a five-foot grid was laid down and adhered to slavishly. Not at all; there are many subtleties and adaptations throughout. But the basic design thinking, so to speak, was done in five-foot increments and from them,

*A Roman foot was a little shorter than ours, about 11⅝ inches, or 0·295 metres.

elaborations and freer modulations were evolved. For example, the corner columns are slightly thicker than the others, following classical precedent, and there are many perspective corrections in the carved detail of the marble entablatures. This classicism and craftsmanship seem to be contradicted by the colorism and baroque qualities of the orders themselves, but this is normal in fully-developed imperial architecture. Greek and Vitruvian traditions were followed, but in forms and materials that belonged to neither. The columns, weighing about forty-eight tons each, are unfluted. They are of tinted granite, and their bases and capitals are of white marble, in all a most un-classical treatment. The entasis is such that its curve becomes flatter toward the ends of each column shaft, another rather baroque quality. Sober as the porch is in contrast to the treatment of the interior of the rotunda, it has many features that are as typically Roman as its relationship to the long axial forecourt.

The porch capitals, the same in design as those inside the rotunda [69 and 70], are of the multi-leaved Corinthian type, and the en-tablatures rise through mouldings, brackets, and rosettes to the cornices that frame them in front and the other lines of the roof roundabout. The fastigium sculpture is unknown. It was natural to have thought that it contained a figural group, but recently it has been suggested that it carried the imperial eagle, settling into a ribboned wreath, wings still spread [71–3], a composition well known in the iconography of Roman dominion. This idea is based upon a careful study of the holes for affixing the décor that exist in the now unfeatured triangle of stone. At the apex of the pediment are the remains of a base for a crowning feature, but what that may have been one can only guess [74].

The flank columns of the porch are met, at the intermediate block, by beautifully-wrought marble pilasters [6]. These continue on the outside of the block and die out against the rotunda; between these there was elaborate marble veneering. Above, behind the porch roof, the otherwise unfeatured block carries a pediment that echoes the one below [12]. From the base of this upper pediment, a cornice runs along the flanks of the block and then out and around the rotunda; the same thing happens with the level cornice at the top of the block. But the marble entablature of the porch does not go beyond the block flanks and, like the pilasters below, ends at the exterior rotunda surface. The lowest of the three rotunda cornices does the same thing in reverse, for it terminates at the pilaster zone of the intermediate block [7]. The manner in which the brickwork of the rotunda was treated is uncertain. It may well have been veneered, or stuccoed, or

69 and 70. The Pantheon: (*above*) interior niche capital; (*below*) interior niche pilaster capital.

71. Dougga, Tunisia,
fastigium of the Forum temple,
late 160s.

72 (*left*). Ephesos, Turkey,
fastigium with a wreath.

73 (*below left*). Palazzo di Giustizia,
Rome, fastigium on the south flank,
c. 1905.

74 (*below right*). The Pantheon,
porch roof from atop
the intermediate block.

75. Ostia, detail of cornice of theater with stucco remaining (right).

76. Model of the Pantheon formerly displayed in the Metropolitan Museum of Art in New York.

covered with the one in the lowest zone and the other above. Attempts at rendering its original appearance rest on minimal evidence. But the three cornices are another matter. Their terracotta and stone elements were originally coated with stucco [75], and they were and are crucial in the definition of the building's shape. They give shadow and articulation to the vast, seamless surface and so make it clearer and more comprehensible to the senses than it would be without them [25]. With cornices, shadow is nearly everything, and in a fundamental way shadow *is* architectural design. It explains the orders and their use, through millennia and in every kind of building, every bit as much as structural necessity does. In the model once displayed in the Metropolitan Museum of Art in New York City, the cornices appear to be subordinated to an overgrowth of detail that the original building probably never carried [76]. The model is of a building in the style of the romantic classicism of the nineteenth century, an important style in its own right but with few connections with Roman imperial architecture; the model-maker could only produce what in his time that architecture was thought to be.

With the long sweep of the forecourt and the stable forms of the porch with its triangular pediment, the architect created the suggestion of a continuing interior longitudinal axis that in fact did not exist. He did what his predecessor at Mycenae had done nearly fifteen hundred years before, combined in plan the straight line and the circle, the straight line being a direct extension of a radius. The hierarchy of forms to the north of the rotunda brought one through sure and familiar ground, up to the moment of gaining the bronze doors at the back of the porch. There the grand north-south axis of the court and porch was dissipated and lost in an incommensurable void. The files of towering vertical forms, passed while traversing the porch, also worked toward the same effect, contrasting powerfully with the wholly different kind of architecture within the rotunda. Thus what appeared from the outside to be quite traditional design led to its antithesis, a revelation of another world. This was effected also by the change in light. The bright, stone-built open court gave way to the relatively dim porch, darker toward its farther reaches. Within the rotunda the lighting was reversed, again becoming full and unimpeded.

To all of this, the chief key is the extraordinary combination of the porch, carrying all the religious implications inherent in its traditional forms, with the rotunda. This had not been done before. The argument sometimes advanced, that the origins of this combination lie in those rectilinear religious buildings whose porches were on the longer sides, will not do. The mere fact that in both cases, say in Agrippa's Pantheon and in Hadrian's, the cella is wider than the porch, gives little help and misses the major point, the use of the vast domed rotunda in place of a rectangular, trabeated cella. In all the Roman architecture that has come down to us, whether fragments or fairly well-preserved buildings, there seems to be only one remote precedent, a tholos temple (Temple B) in a square in Rome, due south of the Pantheon, called the Largo Argentina [77, cf. 20]. Only its podium and a few fragments of columns and walls remain [78], and it was rebuilt from time to time. The original tholos, probably of the mid second century B.C., was altered some time in the first century B.C. by the addition of a four-columned porch. The details are obscure, and the building was again changed in the next century. Apparently the porch was simply brought forward from the ring colonnade of the tholos, where four columns were removed for access to the interior. The podium was also extended in the traditional way, its arms flanking the six or more steps that led up from the precinct pavement. Other than Temple B, there seems to be nothing but inspiration to adduce in explanation of this crucial aspect of the design of the Pantheon.

Relationships between the circle and the square, one aspect of which was noted above, played an important part in Roman architectural design, as did, obviously, the radii of circles and, less obviously, the diagonals of squares and therefore the square root of two. The rotunda is based upon the circle and square relationship: the dome rises from a height above the paving that is exactly equal to its own height, so that in vertical section the rotunda is composed of half of a circle inscribed in the upper half of a square. In other words, the radius of the dome, approximately 75 Roman feet, is the same as the interior height of the cylinder, which is 150 feet in diameter measured from the center of a niche column to that of one opposite. Extended into three dimensions, the theoretical evolution of the interior surfaces of the rotunda is that of half of a sphere – the dome – and a cylinder – the inner vertical wall below – all inscribed in and tangent to the surfaces of an enclosing cube [33]. If that theoretical cube were sliced horizontally across its exact middle, the plane produced would be that from which the dome springs. Vitruvius, who wrote on architecture in Agrippa's day, had speculated about proportions in both architecture and the human figure, and their sympathetic relationships, in something quite like these circle-and-square terms: Leonardo da Vinci's drawing of these Vitruvian suppositions is famous [79]. In it, reciprocities are suggested between the circle and the square, on the one hand, and the reach and theoretical spatial envelope of an

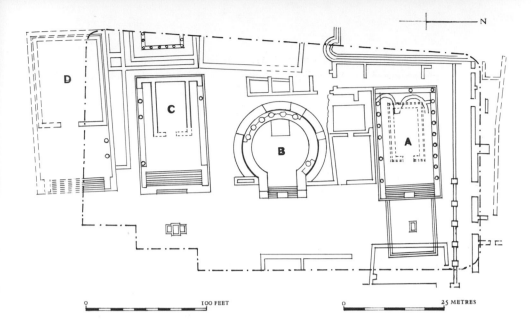

77 and 78. The Largo Argentina, Rome: (*top*) plan of Republican temples, and detail of Temple B.

idealized human figure, on the other. These concepts appear dramatic-
ally enlarged in the Pantheon, where the sweep of the limbs of the
Vitruvian figure are expanded to colossal dimensions. This sympathy
between the forms of Roman vaulted architecture and the spatial
potential of the human figure is perhaps one of the principal keys to
understanding the long life and continuing influence of that architecture [34 and 80].

These broad considerations of design gave generalized forms upon
which the very significant articulation of the interior was wrought.
In the lowest of the zones of the interior, that closest to the observer
and most readily comprehensible, it will be seen that, while circular,
the wall also advances and retreats in a symmetrical system of
aediculae and niches right and left of the unemphasized axis connecting
the entrance with the apse [11 and 81]. The result is a quality that
can properly be called baroque, that is, dramatic, filled with light and
shade, and rich with the energy of breaking forward and pulling back,
in the manner of the stage-buildings of second-century Roman
theaters [82]. It is the opposite of a plain, unfeatured wall. The use of
colored marbles for the orders and veneer adds to this baroque quality.
This is not the full baroque of the seventeenth century [83], but it is a
great distance, in terms of visual qualities and emotional power, from
the regularly repeated rhythms and cool clarity of the classical
architecture of Greek temples or, say, the colonnades of the Pantheon
forecourt. Here, in the first zone, the sizes of the orders vary and the
spaces between vertical elements widen and narrow in regular
rhythms. The center spaces between the niche columns are wider
than their flanking spaces. These factors, combined with the advance
and retreat of the numerous elements and surfaces, and with the
light and shade of the whole, create effects that have little or nothing
to do with the sober, lucid effects of the Greek masters of centuries
before. Here columns support little, for they are used to contrive
effects quite different from those structural functions which columns
originally expressed. The actual work of supporting the building is
done by masses of unseen concrete, and the architect used his classic-
ally-wrought orders for what can only be called unclassical purposes.

This more purely visual, indeed cosmetic, use of the orders is a
hallmark of Roman imperial architecture. The Greeks had done it,
to be sure, but sparingly and never in a riot of colors. The new Roman
technology of building invited it, as did of course the desire to create
illusions of tinted atmospheres, of shells of colored space. The structure
of a building, so beautifully displayed in a classical Doric temple,
had in much Roman imperial design withdrawn behind a surface

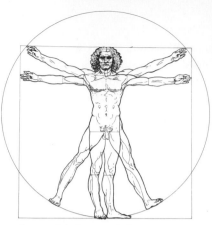

79. Leonardo's interpretation
of the Vitruvian man, redrawn.

80. Nero's Golden House, Rome,
detail of the octagonal atrium.

81. The Pantheon, interior, seen from the west transverse niche.

82. Sabratha, Libya,
model of the theater stage-building.

83. S. Maria in Campitelli, Rome,
upper part of the façade, 1662–7.

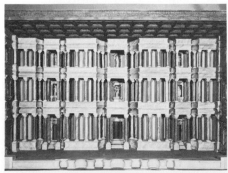

architecture of no structural significance. Walls and vaults were, by the second century, not yet dematerialized as in, say, such a master-piece of proto-Byzantine architecture as the fifth-century Orthodox Baptistery in Ravenna [118], but the process was well under way.

These tendencies can be seen in the way the great niches are screened by colored marble columns. The effect is not that of archi-tectural clarity, but the opposite. The columns seem to be helping to hold up the high solid wall above, while in fact unseen vaults and concrete do this work [4 and 26]. Behind the columns are darkish recesses, their nature necessarily obscured somewhat by the columns in front of them; something of a sense of mystery, or at least of ambiguity, is induced by all of this. The polished marble surfaces of the first two zones, by reflecting light and making their substance hard to gauge, help to reduce the sense of the existence of the massive structure behind. The present decoration of the attic storey, quite matte in contrast to the marbles of the first zone, which them-selves have been dulled by time, helps to make this point. In the attic zone, the robust moldings emphasize the blind windows much more than the original scheme would have done, and a sense of weight, mass, and structure is expressed much more obviously than in the zone below. Above, in the zone of the dome, the idea of expanding space, expressed by the niches, was continued and confirmed by the use of perspective coffers.

In the two lower zones, the positioning of the major architectural forms was determined by dividing the circle of the plan first into quarters, then into eighths, and so on. The architectural elements of the décor of the second zone were vertically matched with those of the lower one. But this congruity is abandoned in the dome, where there are twenty-eight radial rows of coffers, a function of seven and fourteen rather than of four, eight, and so on. Thus the coffer system will not synchronize with the verticals of the zones below, except along the four cardinal axes, and this adds a certain restlessness to the design. It is hard to say what reason there may have been for this, but if there had been sixteen or thirty-two radial rows of coffers, the building would have had a more fixed and static presence. It may be that the sizes of coffers that would have resulted from using sixteen or thirty-two rows would have been out of scale with the rest of the elements of design. Suggestions that the number twenty-eight relates to the days of the week and the length of the lunar month are interesting, but probably cannot be carried any useful distance.

The perspective composition of the coffers enlivens the effect of the interior. It is only at or near the center of the pavement that all surfaces

84. The Pantheon, shadows on the dome coffers.

of all coffers are revealed to the observer. Seen from other positions the edges of the pyramidal boxes begin to overlap, their recesses suggesting a greater depth than the hemisphere actually has: the principle is related to the screening effect of the niche columns. As the light angles in, the surfaces of the coffers are revealed in a complex pattern of varying degrees of light and shade. Often a pattern is formed by the fuller illumination of the triangular portions of the coffers below their diagonals, intimating a curving sweep of expanding lines like those formed by the sparks spun out from a pinwheel [84]. One is reminded of the mosaic pavements, popular in Hadrianic times, of Medusa heads enframed by a swirl of curves [85]. In these, the head

85. Mosaic in the National Museum, Rome.

appears in a central, comparatively small circle, around which ever larger circles are set. These circles are traversed by curved lines running from the central medallion to the periphery of the whole, creating a powerful illusion of looking into a deep whirling space toward its vortex.

Natural light in the building is quite uniform, save for the disc of much higher intensity that moves through the northern half of the building as the day passes. At the summer solstice this path is approximately as follows:

74

at 9 a.m. the disc is at position 14 in the attic zone, reaching up slightly above the second cornice, and tangent to the upper surface of the cornice below.

at 10 a.m. it reaches from the lower cornice to the pavement, shining on the right-hand half of the aedicula at position 14 and reaching over to the left-hand column and part of the interior of the niche at 15.

at 11 a.m. it is entirely on the floor of the building, reaching from the middle of 15 to the middle of 16, and tangent to the rotunda wall.

at noon it has moved almost due east to a place on the pavement between the middle of 16 and the middle of 1, its northernmost limit some nine feet from the inner west corner of the entrance bay.

at 1 p.m. it is on the pavement at the base of 3.

at 3 p.m. it is on the attic zone just a little to the left of the center line of 5.

at 4 p.m. it is more or less centered around the lowest coffer above position 5.

at 5 p.m. it has climbed well up into the dome and is more or less centered on the coffer of the third ring in the vertical file, one to the right of that rising above position 5.

As the earth continues to rotate, the brilliant disc, its shape altering as it travels along the hemispherical surface, slips rapidly over the uppermost coffers. With increasing speed it moves along the last, smooth portion of the dome, and then suddenly it disappears, as if it had been drawn abruptly out through the oculus.

4

THE PROBLEM
OF
MEANING

To say with any precision what the Pantheon meant to Hadrian and his contemporaries will probably never be possible. There are several reasons for this, among them the lack of written evidence from the period, the inevitable subjectivity involved in analysis of the meaning of architectural form, the state of our knowledge of Roman imperial society and its attitudes, and the disadvantages of hindsight. In spite of these formidable barriers the attempt is worth making again – it has been made a number of times before – because of the importance of the building both in its own time and later.

The positive data are few. Dedications to all the gods were not uncommon; there had been several such sanctuaries in Greek lands, though Agrippa's seems to have been the first in Rome. It has been held that the word Pantheon meant most holy, or very holy, but this is unlikely in view of the one relevant ancient textual passage we have. This is found in a history of Rome written by Dio Cassius, a civil servant who rose to the consulship in the early third century :

> Also he [Agrippa] completed the building called the Pantheon. It has this name, perhaps because it received among the images which decorate it the statues of many gods, including Mars and Venus; but my opinion of the name is that, because of its vaulted roof, it resembles the heavens. Agrippa, for his part, wished to place a statue of Augustus there also and to bestow upon him the honor of having the structure named after him; but when the emperor would not accept either honor, he placed in the temple itself a statue of the former Caesar [i.e. Julius] and in the porch statues of Augustus and himself. This was done, not out of any rivalry or ambition on Agrippa's part to make himself equal to Augustus, but from his hearty loyalty to him and his constant zeal for the public good; hence Augustus, so far from censuring him for it, honored him the more.

Obviously Dio believed Hadrian's building to be Agrippa's, and it is clear that in Dio's day the Pantheon contained, among other statues, those of Mars and Venus. The presence of a statue of Venus in Agrippa's Pantheon is confirmed by a first-century text, and it seems very probable that the three other statues Dio mentioned could still be seen, in his day, in the porch or rotunda. Though the sentences about Augustus and Agrippa might conceivably have come from pre-Hadrianic sources used by Dio, the balance is strongly in favor of saying that Hadrian's building contained at least the images of Mars, Venus, and Julius Caesar, and that there were statues of Augustus and Agrippa outside, presumably set in the two great niches of the intermediate block. Where Dio's 'statues of many gods' were located, and what gods they represented, is not known. It is tempting to try to match the images of fifteen of the senior gods and goddesses with the apse, the niches, and the aediculae, or to fit the seven ancient planetary deities to the six niches and the apse, but there is no real basis for such proceedings. The interior disposition of figural sculpture remains as vague as the dedication to all gods; conjecture reigns. Finally, with respect to Dio's remarks, it is significant that the statues of many gods were by no means the only images that decorated the building.

Certainly the gods were there, ranged in the niches and aediculae of the interior, facing one on all sides. More than that cannot be said. Agrippa's caryatids, which would have been jarringly out of place in Hadrian's building, had surely vanished. What we perhaps most need to know about the meaning of the Pantheon, the gods' names and positions, is lost, in all likelihood forever. So too, probably, is the reason for its unusual orientation to the north.

But Dio's passage can start another hare, one well worth following. He says that Agrippa put a statue of Julius Caesar, who had been deified only a decade or two earlier, inside the original Pantheon, together with images of Mars, Venus, and others. The entry of the Deified Julius into the Pantheon associated Augustus' family directly with the gods, for Augustus was Julius' great-nephew and adopted son. With Augustus' refusal to have his own image put inside the building, it was made clear that the shrine proper could contain effigies only of gods, as the dedication would require. But these gods did not necessarily have to be solely the ancient and traditional ones, for 'all gods' could and did include deities of recent origin and, so to speak, of comparatively low rank. By putting the Deified Julius inside, Augustus was given a connection with the gods, for whom he stood guard outside with Agrippa, his great minister and friend. Seen in this light, the original Pantheon takes on a strong dynastic and political coloring.

It was a monument composed as much of political and personal factors as of religious ones. Augustus is renowned for such programs; major works of Augustan art celebrate them. It is possible, even likely, that the original Pantheon was Augustus' idea.

There is ample evidence to show that although he only gradually permitted formal worship of himself, he was by no means loath to be represented, at any time, near or among the gods. The most useful and telling example of this for our purposes is the spacious new Forum that Augustus dedicated in Rome in 2 B.C. [86 and 87]. There was a good deal of Hellenistic precedent for official works of art associating a ruler with the gods, as well as for ruler-worship proper. The Augustan monarchy was inevitably derived, in substantial ways, from Hellenistic practice, and sought to promote the claims of the non-despotic autocrat by all persuasive means. In the east, Augustus could be hailed openly as a god; in Rome a more subdued and less direct approach was required.

A fair amount of the Forum remains, and there are inscriptions, texts, and fragments of sculpture that record additional aspects of its original appearance. The nature and intent of its architecture and its program of images, that is, its iconography, are quite clear. The white marble architectural décor and detailing were mostly of direct classical and Hellenistic inspiration, cool and very elegant [88 and 89]. The plan was more Roman. There was, on the model of the nearby Forum of Julius Caesar, a long paved forecourt flanked by stoas, at the end of which stood a very large temple to Mars Ultor (Mars the Avenger, the avenger of the murdered Julius). Behind the stoas, at the temple end, and dilating outward from the main rectangular space, were two symmetrical curved wings or exedrae. The entire complex was decorated with a profusion of statuary, clearly of patriotic and dynastic implications, as tendentiously Augustan as his famous propagandistic recitation, known from inscriptions, of 'the things I accomplished [in my reign]'. In the many niches of the stoas and exedrae [90 and 91], one saw the images of Aeneas, Romulus, the ancient kings of Rome and of Alba Longa (the legendary home of the Julian house), famous ancestors of Julius and Augustus, and many other great Romans of the past. Above the eight fluted marble Corinthian columns of the temple façade, Mars stood at the center of the triangular fastigium, flanked by Venus, Fortuna, Romulus again, and Roma [92]. In the acute angles were representations of Father Tiber and the Palatine, the hill where, legend had it, Rome was founded so long ago. Augustus' name presumably appeared prominently on the entablature below. Out in the Forum proper there was a gilded bronze quadriga, a four-

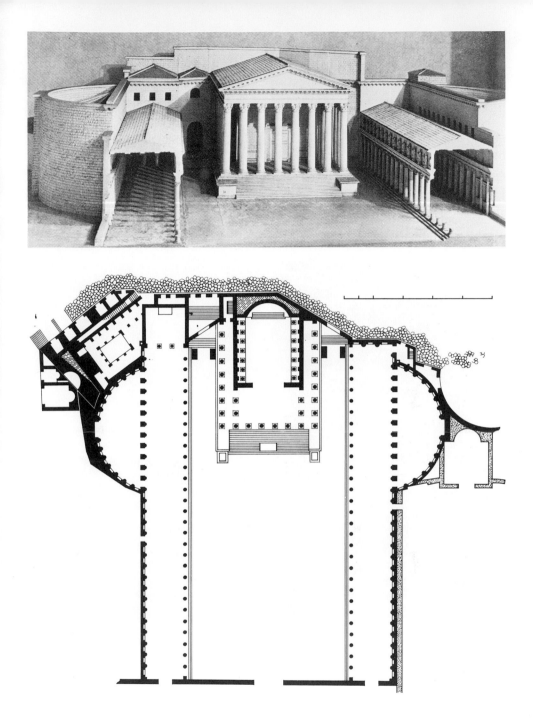

86 and 87. Forum of Augustus, Rome, dedicated 2 B.C.: model and plan.

88. Forum of Augustus, Rome, marblework.

89. Forum of Augustus, Rome, pilaster.

90. Forum of Augustus, Rome, exedra.

91. Forum of Augustus, Rome, exedra niches.

92. Forum of Augustus, Rome,
plan showing probable locations of statues.

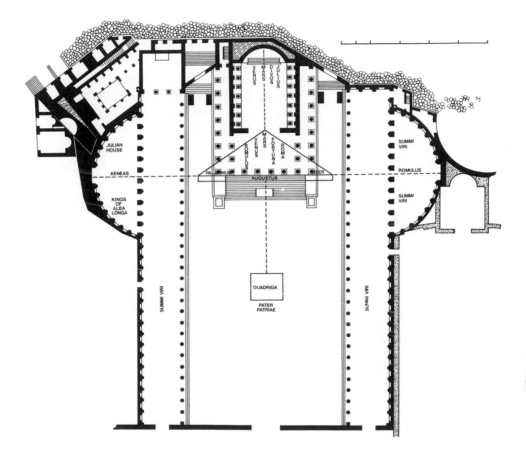

horse chariot, in whose car the emperor's image stood. By analogy with other monuments, it is possible to believe that this was in the center of the open paving, about half-way between the temple and the axial entrance to the Forum. Beyond, inside the cella of the temple, images of Mars the titular deity, Venus the ancestress of the Julian house, and the Deified Julius kept watch. Perhaps all three stood in the wide, curving apse at the end.

Because the new Forum stood next to the Forum of Caesar, its manifest filial and pious claims were strengthened. It was completely enclosed by a lofty and powerful wall, that stood even higher at the back of the temple, where the land began to rise fairly steeply [93]. Thus, unlike the sprawling, ancient Republican forum nearby, it was a place where one's attention, vision, and path were severely restricted. The Temple of Mars on its high podium [94] nearly filled the space between the parallel stoas, and control over the viewer by means of the enclosed, one-ended plan was enhanced by the great wall behind the temple that delimited the composition absolutely. This great wall served also as the back of the temple, and rose well above the ridge line of the temple roof [87]. Below, the flank colonnades died out against it, so the temple had no visible fourth, rear side [94]. Thus the Forum was an interior, in the sense that the outside world was excluded and, of nature, only the sky could be seen. One's senses, once one had passed through the portals of the towering enclosure wall, could react only to what was there, and what was there was Augustan rhetoric in architecture; there were no distractions whatsoever.

By 2 B.C., when the Forum was dedicated, Agrippa had been dead for ten years, but his – or his master's – concept of the assimilation of the imperial imagery into a sacred place in Rome itself was still very much alive. Even the idea of using caryatids was copied from the Pantheon for use on the stoas of the Forum [95]. Augustus managed to combine in one grand public monument everything of peace and war, of politics and traditional society, of religion and patriotism, and to link them directly with his name and deeds and with those of his family: he had avenged Julius' death, and he had brought his peace to war-weary nations. By drawing on such sources of eastern sanctuaries dedicated to Hellenistic rulers, the ancient and powerful symbolism of the temple and its fastigium, and the design of Julius' forum, his architects and artists created for him a monumental exhibition of the allied religious and dynastic foundations claimed for the new world monarchy.

The same spirit and objectives underlie the program of the celebrated Ara Pacis Augustae, the Altar of Augustan Peace, begun in 9 B.C.

93. Forum of Augustus, Rome, the great wall behind the Temple of Mars Ultor.

94. Forum of Augustus, Rome, remains of the Temple of Mars Ultor.

95. Forum of Augustus, Rome, caryatids and relief sculpture from a stoa attic.

There Aeneas, allegorical figures, Vestal Virgins, senators, and symbols of the plenty gained through Augustan rule appear together with figures of the emperor, his family and advisors. Some of his other dynastic and political monuments carry the same message, partly taken, again, from Hellenistic sources, but fashioned to his purposes. Virgil joined in the praise of empire and ruler as did other writers. By the time of Augustus' death in 14, when half or more of the people then alive in the vast Greco-Roman world had never known any other prince, the pattern was set. Gods and rulers, the state and its claims, could be and were given at one important level of meaning a loosely knit but common identity. The slack in that looseness was to be taken up gradually in the future. The Augustan monarchy, once defined as the least unjust of governments, was transformed over the centuries into an undisguised and orientalized despotism, a despotism that for survival had to claim that the gods, the ruler, and the state were all but identical. In Augustus' time, however, the association of these powerful forces on a common level was only suggested, and in his new Forum this suggestion was offered with some subtlety through the agency of sufficiently traditional architectural and sculptural forms. What was suggested might draw the fire of conservatives and republicans, but it seems clear that to most people the message was palatable and to many only right and fitting.

The general correspondence between the Forum of Augustus and Hadrian's Pantheon parallels that of the tombs of the two men [46 and 47]. Irrespective of differences of form, particularly the difference between the Temple of Mars and the Pantheon rotunda, there are numerous and striking similarities between the two monuments. By affixing Agrippa's inscription to his building, Hadrian celebrated its Augustan ancestry. This, so naturally assumed in modern times to be a deliberately disingenuous act, can in combination with other evidence be read as a clue pointing firmly to Hadrian's Augustan model. In this regard, it is to the point that Dio Cassius, when referring to the images in the rotunda, singled out as worth identifying by name those same three gods whose images stood in the cella of the Temple of Mars Ultor. In any event, we know that both monuments housed, among others, the same major images, and that the façade inscriptions of both spoke of the Augustan age. Taken alone, these things might not mean much, but there is more.

Consider, first, the general principles of axial design and the resulting sequence of forms and visual events. There is something here of Hellenistic principles, come to Rome by way of such monuments as the Forum of Julius Caesar, but this common ancestry only makes the bond between the two designs the more firm. In each case, an axial main entrance gave on to a long rectangular forecourt containing, in the one case, a triumphal arch, in the other, perhaps, the imperial quadriga [15 and 92]. Beyond each a temple loomed, its size magnified by the lesser scale of forecourt colonnades. In each case, the termination of the entire design was obscured by a temple façade that filled one's vision. What was at the end of the axis could not be inferred by the ordinary observer, and the exterior of that end of the composition was of no consequence, indeed could not be, in view of the visual principles of the whole. The south end of the Pantheon rotunda was the mere exterior shell of a grand space, in itself of no meaning. The end wall of the Temple of Mars was so placed as to eliminate the far end of that building entirely. Although that area of the Augustan plan was asymmetrical, apparently because of pre-existing landlines and terrain, one could not tell this without going all the way to the ends of the two stoas, separated by the huge temple, and comparing them. Symmetry was contrived because it had to be : the imperial message was order itself.

Both temple fronts were deep, both *octastyle* (eight-columned), and both had two interior files of columns back toward the enclosed structure beyond, rotunda or cella. Behind each porch, closer in the Pantheon than in the Temple of Mars, stood high vertical features of rectangular silhouette, the Augustan enclosing wall and the inter-mediate block. The cella of the Temple of Mars was almost square in plan, that is, very broad in terms of the traditional canon. It was finished with an apse as wide as the distance between its interior colonnades, which were set close in front of responding pilasters on the cella walls. There were seven columns on each side, between which were niches of rectangular plan. This cella plan was to the plan of the Pantheon rotunda — leaving aside for the moment the difference in size and roofing — what the fluted marble columns of the Temple façade were to the smooth granite shafts of the Pantheon porch, the differences being accounted for by the architectural evolution sketched in the previous chapter. Both spaces had columns, niches, and an apse, set in volumes as broad as they were long.

The principle of enclosure, so important to the design and meaning of the Forum of Augustus, applies to the Pantheon ensemble as well and, of course, to the rotunda in particular. The rotunda, however, is much more closely related to the Forum than that. Truly exact measure-ments are hard to obtain, and the results of the excavation of the Forum some forty years ago have never been published in any detail. However, the exedrae [87 and 90], which are segments of circles subtending about $155°$, have radii seventy-five feet in length, taken to the inner faces of their niched walls; the Pantheon rotunda's cylinder and dome were also generated from this same measurement. The façade of the Temple of Mars lies exactly on the transverse axis upon which the exedrae are centered, and the extension of the exedrae curves produces circles tangent to the corner columns of the Temple. Finally, in respect of the exedrae, both had a deep, central niche, flanked on each side in turn by seven smaller, shallower niches which, if the exedrae were half round in plan, would be eight in number. It seems entirely possible that, in important respects, the design of the Pantheon rotunda was an elaboration of the plan of the Forum exedrae, both in respect of size and of the division of the cylinder wall, while the porch set against the intermediate block clearly echoed the Temple of Mars set against its high backing wall.

There are other connections. The outside diameter of the Pantheon rotunda is the same as the width of the Forum between its stoa colonnades. The walls of the stoas and those of the exedrae were highly articulated, not only by niches, but also by the marble half-columns engaged to them [91]. The Temple cella walls were even more baroque, with their free-standing columns, responding pilasters and niches. In the Forum, colored marbles were used, among them the giallo antico and pavonazzetto so prominent inside the Pantheon rotunda. Chiefly, however, the Forum orders were of white marble and, as mentioned above, of beautiful workmanship in the classical tradition, probably from the hands of Greek craftsmen. In a standing portion of the right hand gallery of the Temple (the space between the cella and its exterior, flanking colonnade), the original marble coffering is in place: the sides of the enboxed frames are slanted inward, on a pyramidal system [96].

Though some of these relationships merely connect both monuments with Roman architecture in general, the number and nature of their correspondences brings them a good deal closer. There is much in the Pantheon, in design as in iconography, that quite probably was derived from the Forum of Augustus. The century and a quarter that separates them accounts for many of their differences. The intent remains quite constant, although Hadrian inevitably added more and complex strains of meaning to the comparatively simple framework of Augustan purpose. As architectural conceptions, however, they are very similar.

The architectural vocabulary employed by Hadrian's designer was a mixture of the traditional and the creative. The major external parts of his composition could be read as familiar symbols. The fore-

96. Forum of Augustus, Rome, coffering of the Temple of Mars Ultor.

court with its stoas and arch spoke of the traditions of the Mediterranean colonnaded street and of the triumphant qualities of Roman-
ness, while of all the orders the Corinthian was, during the empire, by
far the most representative of things Roman. The ancient religious
message of the porch was self-evident, but if in fact there was an
imperial eagle in the fastigium, that most sacred of architectural forms,
the alliance of government and gods would have been very strongly
expressed indeed. But all this imagery was familiar, and its meaning
obvious, to the ancient observer. The interior of the rotunda, however,
was quite different. Its potential of meaning will be discussed here
under three headings: its intimations of dominion; its allusions to
the planetary mystery; and light, the engine of its most evocative yet
intangible effects.

The idea of an enclosed architectural volume pierced through the
roof for light and air went back to earliest times. In one evolution it

had resulted in the inward-looking atrium house, so familiar from Pompeii, where rooms were symmetrically disposed around a central, larger space lit by a fairly good-sized roof-opening. In another, intersecting the new concrete technology, it appeared in such vaulted rotundas as the so-called Temple of Mercury at Baia [52]. In the Pantheon, that aspect of the design was old, the scale and purpose breathtakingly new. The empire was immense, watched over by all the gods, and the imperial system claimed, if not perfection, success and permanence. Order and the system were synonymous, and the most orderly of geometric, and therefore of architectural, shapes is the circle. It is without corners and without seams, and has no beginning and no end. It stands for continuity and, when raised in form to a great height and vaulted over, it intimates an inclusive security. In a very real sense, the Pantheon rotunda is a metaphor in architecture for the ecumenical pretensions of the Roman Empire, the girdling cornices a statement in architectural form of the nine-thousand-mile boundary that surrounded the later Greco-Roman world, the world of which the Roman government at its best felt itself to be the steward. The Pantheon rotunda, its entrance gained by passing along and through the traditional architectural forms of that world, revealed a great symbol of the dominion of Rome in one poignant visual experience. The theme, of course, was unity – the unity of gods and state, of people and state, and the unity of the perpetual existence and function of the state with the never-ending revolutions of the planetary clockwork. The grid underfoot, in appearance like the Roman surveyor's plan for a town [35], appeared overhead in the coffering, up in the zone of the mysteries of the heavens. To unify unities is to produce the universal, and this is perhaps the Pantheon's ultimate meaning.

One of the main characteristics of the culture of the High Empire has been shown to be an increasing syncretism of religious beliefs, at the expense of traditional religion, the gradual depreciation of which was sometimes based on quasi-science, sometimes on the subjective pursuit of classically-based philosophy. With Mithraism and Christianity, the peoples of the empire were deeply involved in teachings that made far more of a world unseen than of this one. In a sense, the world had come close to the point of the exhaustion of its ancient spiritual resources. For many people, high and low, the old explanations and interpretations would not do. One of the most important things about the Pantheon is that it was created at this time, at a turning point in history, when rites and rules drawn from a very long past were not yet abandoned, but when the surge of a new and utterly different age was already being felt. Because of this the Pantheon is suffused with a quality of seeking, in the sense that it did not fit into the traditional frame of architectural expression and experience. Its forms record an attempt to describe something of the awe in which man has always held the universe, visible and invisible, something of man both insignificant and meaningful. It is truly a building of immanence, of no firmly held and dogmatically expressed religious belief.

It is perhaps reasonable to suppose that the planetary deities were represented, however hopeless the task may be of trying to assign them places in the rotunda. They were Mercury, Mars, Venus, Jupiter, the Moon, the Sun, and Saturn; for many people they stood for Tyche or Fortune as well. The shape of the building, the disk of light, the seven major niches (including the apse), and the astrological and quasi-astronomical preoccupations of the times make it possible, if not necessarily probable, that representations of the planets were present. What seems more certain is that the dome was intended as a symbol of the heavens, the abode of the gods, ruled over by Zeus-Jupiter, the Sky God and Sky Father. His place, if not marked by an image in the rotunda, was the void seen through the oculus. Dio thought that the heavens were the key to understanding the Pantheon, and he was far closer to the thought and religious attitudes of Hadrian's time than any other person whose observations about the building we have.

All the gods, then; part of a cosmology expressed in architecture, sculpture, and light, placed in Rome by Hadrian, the Father of his People. The intimate connection of the forces of the cosmos with the ruler and his subjects found frequent expression not only in official monuments, but also in humbler forms. A papyrus records part of a dramatic performance played in an Egyptian town on the occasion of Hadrian's accession:

> I have just risen on high with Trajan
> in my white-horsed chariot.
> I come to you, people,
> the god Phoebus — whom you know —
> to proclaim Hadrian as the new ruler
> whom all things serve for his ability
> and the genius of his Divine Father, gladly.

Phoebus is Apollo in his capacity as the sun-god, appearing on the stage. Trajan, deified, is in heaven with the gods, and Hadrian, his son

97. The Pantheon, view through the bronze doors.

by imperial succession and therefore the son of a god, has become the ruler of all things. An audience that took all this as a matter of course would not have found the meaning of the Pantheon elusive. The implications of Phoebus' speech and the message expressed by the imagery of the Pantheon were one and the same.

Order, peace, harmony, unity — these were the immediate meanings of the Pantheon, cast in a religious setting. And it was a kind of orrery as well, in which planetary implications were signalled directly as the earth revolved. Zeus-Jupiter-Helios, the supreme god allied with the Great Sun, was himself inside the rotunda, his effulgence visible but intangible. The sun, said the ancients, is the eye of Zeus, and in Hadrian's Pantheon the greatest of the gods was epiphanized in light. Above all it is the garment of light worn by the rotunda which connects the individual with the heavens, and which, appearing in movement on the architecture, bridges the intangible and the tangible [97]. The long cylinder of light that is shaped by the oculus and pries through the building is one of the triumphs in architecture of the expression of a world-feeling, a triumph that belongs to Hadrian [98].

98. The Pantheon, dome and oculus.

Thus the Pantheon expresses central currents affecting and defining the human condition of the time. It was not a temple in the traditional sense of a barn-like form, for religious architecture had moved away from that (very few major traditional temples would be built in the remaining two centuries of the pre-Christian empire). Hadrian even held judicial court in the rotunda. Plainly, no single word will fit all these facts except universality. In its curves the Pantheon suggests universality in two ways: the circular paths of the planets under the dome of heaven, and an ideated circumference of the universal empire. The rotunda stands for the claim of a unified, perfected, seamless, comprehensible whole – the order of the empire, sanctioned and watched over by the gods.

Of the many descriptions of its nature and effects, three are particularly evocative:

It is as it were the visible image of the universe; in the perfection of its proportions, as when you regard the unmeasured dome of Heaven, the idea of magnitude is swallowed up & lost. It is open to the sky, & its wide dome is lighted by the ever changing illumination of the air. The clouds of noon fly over it and at night the keen stars are seen thro the azure darkness hanging immoveably, or driving after the driven moon among the clouds. (Shelley)

The form of the house of the image was the form of the cosmos with man at its center. The shape of space was the shape of a perfect circle as the base of a perfect sphere, the circle of the Empire's horizon under the dome of its firmament. (Frank E. Brown)

On the same day, with graver solemnity, as if muted, a dedicatory ceremony took place inside the Pantheon . . . My intention had been that this Sanctuary of All Gods should reproduce the likeness of the terrestrial globe and of the stellar sphere, that globe wherein are enclosed the seeds of eternal fire, and that hollow sphere containing all. Such was also the form of our ancestors' huts where the smoke of man's earliest hearths escaped through an orifice at the top. The cupola . . . which still seemed to share in the upward movement of flames, revealed the sky through a great hole at the center, showing alternately dark and blue. This temple, both open and mysteriously enclosed, was conceived as a solar quadrant. The hours would make their round on that caissoned ceiling, so carefully polished by Greek artisans; the disk of daylight would rest suspended there like a shield of gold; rain would form its clear pool on the pavement below; prayers would rise like smoke toward that void where we place the gods. (Marguerite Yourcenar)

Like Trajan's towering column [99], equally universal in its message and equally difficult to interpret with any finality, the Pantheon is an icon of Rome's claims and mission. The two monuments are the most significant creations of Roman art. When they are more fully understood, the real nature of the Age of Rome will not only be better known to us, but more useful, for surely many things of enduring value still lie in them unread.

99. Trajan's Column, Rome, dedicated 113.

5

'THE MOST CELEBRATED EDIFICE'

At the back of the Pantheon porch, just to the right of the great bronze entrance doors and high up on the wall, is an inscription of 1632, placed there by Urban VIII. The first three lines read

PANTHEON
AEDIFICIVM TOTO TERRARVM ORBE
CELEBERRIMVM

'The Pantheon, the most celebrated edifice in the whole world.' How right this is can be seen by leafing through the illustrations of any standard history of architecture, noting how often domed rotundas with temple-front porches appear. These progeny of the Pantheon are ubiquitous, the result more than anything of an all-encompassing imagery expressing universality, that made it possible for the building to be meaningful in different ways in different historical periods. It has always been a symbol of Rome, and of things Roman as they have been variously conceived over the centuries; probably it is the most poignant monumental reminder of that age so long gone. Again and again it has provided inspiration in response to needs unknown when it was built. Unlike the vast palaces, the imperial fora, and the other stupendous works of the Caesars, it has continued to stand. Only the Colosseum might have rivalled it as symbol and paradigm, but the Colosseum was tainted with the spectacular deaths of pagans and Christians it had witnessed. In any event, it was a kind of open structure of which little future architectural use could be made, though in time its exterior design and its technology became important to Renaissance and later architects. Furthermore, the Pantheon is a truly large interior volume, a building whose size seemed all but incommensurable and could not during much of its long existence have been duplicated. This came to stimulate and challenge architects almost as much as its imagery and design, especially from the early Renaissance onward when they began, through detailed measurement and study, to try to decipher its ancient mysteries and make direct use of their findings. Only then did monumental rivals of the Pantheon appear, from the hands of Italian masters.

The image of a domed rotunda rising behind a temple-like entrance-way is ineradicably set in the accumulated visual experience of Western man. An exhaustive discussion of the function of the Pantheon in the history of architecture cannot be attempted here. But certain points stand out; briefly, they are as follows. The first is the curious but fundamental fact that the Pantheon has never been duplicated or copied, at any scale; each Pantheon-like building is, to a greater or lesser degree, a free interpretation of the concepts established in Hadrian's day, its stylistic distance from the original being the inevitable result of the effect of contemporary architectural fashion and prejudice, and the predilections of its architect. Even during the late eighteenth and early nineteenth centuries, when the rage for ancient architecture knew few bounds, no copies were made. The second important point is that the story of the Pantheon in architectural history divides into several clearly differentiated historical phases, the result of particular cultural and stylistic conditions, each phase characterized by an attitude toward the Pantheon that can be defined quite accurately. Each will be discussed below by selecting two or three buildings that represent their period fairly. A third point is that after twin towers were added to the façade in the early seventeenth century [14], architects had an additional theme to deal with. And then there is the vexed question of the source of the original idea for a two-towered façade on a domed rotunda, which was to have such a lively future in architecture. Finally, the means whereby each age learned about the Pantheon are significant, for they help to explain how its didactic role was sustained for so long.

THE LATER ROMAN EMPIRE (c. 150–350)

Later Roman architects continued to explore the exciting potential of vaulted round buildings, which were common east and west. Rethinking the problem brought some spectacular creative successes, while the design of certain building types, notably mausolea, remained conservative as late as the fifth century. Although temple building declined in late antiquity, there are examples in the Pantheon manner, muted in grandeur but of unmistakable origin. The trabeated porch was played down or eliminated and the exterior of the rotunda was

100. The so-called Temple of Diana,
Baia, Hadrianic date;
presumably a hall in a bath building.

101 (*below*). Model of the Baths
of Caracalla, Rome, early third century.

102 (*left*). The Sanctuary of Asklepios,
Pergamon, Turkey, *c.* 145, model.

103 (*below left*). The Temple of Asklepios,
Pergamon, Turkey,
remains of the rotunda wall and apse,
c. 145.

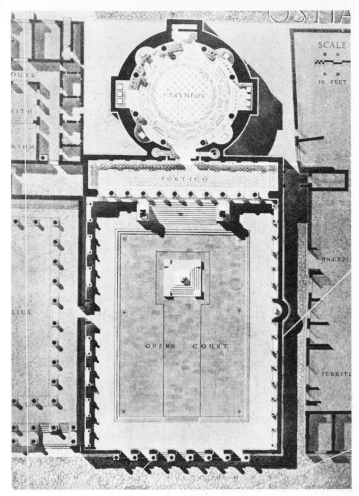

104 and 105.
The Round Temple
at Ostia, 230–40:
plan, and restored view.

increasingly displayed as an architectural form in its own right. Eight-sided and even ten-sided plans appeared. Centralized vaulted rooms continued to be built in bath complexes large and small [100]. Some were huge and projected, not only up above their adjoining halls, but out from them in plan as well, as at the immense baths of Caracalla, in Rome, of the early third century [101]. The building of grand baths all around the Empire continued well into the fourth century and helped to keep the concept of the domed, unobstructed, centralized space, and the technology of its construction, very much alive.

In this first or imperial phase of the Pantheon's life in architecture, temple and tomb design were most influenced. What was apparently the first 'copy' of the Pantheon was a temple to Asklepios Soter of about 145, built in the old Hellenistic city of Pergamon in Asia Minor at a healing center dedicated to the god-physician [102]. The porch had only four columns, the 'intermediate block' was elongated and apparently given a pitched roof, and the interior diameter of the rotunda was eighty Roman feet as opposed to the Pantheon's one hundred and fifty. The cylinder was of cut stone and the dome of brick [103, where part of the fallen vault is visible in the middle distance beyond the apse]. The Pantheon's niches were repeated, but the stairs were put at the back, against the flat stretch of wall behind the apse.

At Ostia, the port city of Rome at the mouth of the Tiber, there are the remains of a somewhat similar structure known as the Round Temple, dating from about 230 or 240 [104 and 105]. Here the porch was widened to fill the breadth of a Pantheon-like court, but there does not seem to be any evidence for a pediment (the plan shown here is basically correct, but the perspective restoration is in some ways conjectural). The rotunda is sixty Roman feet in diameter, and the seven major niches of the Pantheon appear, though of rather different shapes. An important change has taken place, however, for the transverse niches and the apse, expanded to a greater size in relation to the volume of the whole than at the Pantheon, project beyond the exterior wall of the rotunda. This is early evidence of the increasing attention later architects will pay to these niches, in respect of both their relative size and their potential in articulating the exterior wall, which at Ostia, however, has not yet been opened up by windows. Another indication of the heightened interest in the design of the rotunda exterior is the reduction of the intermediate block in the Round Temple to a thickness just sufficient to contain the maintenance staircases. Whatever details may originally have appeared on the exterior, it is clear from the plan that the architect wished, so to speak,

106. The so-called Temple of Romulus, Rome, *c.* 309.

to unmask the rotunda and give it a more emphatic plastic definition than earlier rotundas had.

Another, somewhat smaller version was built in Rome quite early in the fourth century, the so-called Temple of Romulus beside the ancient Sacred Way, toward the eastern end of the republican Forum [106]. It may have been the tomb or shrine of a young prince who died in 309, but no one really knows. There was no room for an axial forecourt, but the building was set back a little from the street, its entrance focused at the center of an incurving wall more or less tangential to the rotunda, a typical late antique device. Above the unpedimented frame around the bronze doors rises a flat, thin, unfeatured reminiscence of the Pantheon's intermediate block. Above that, at the base of the dome, are two step-rings (the little cupola or lantern is not ancient). The whole is rather tall for its width. It shows, as does the Round Temple at Ostia, that the general idea of the Pantheon counted for a good deal in the minds of late antique architects, the exact form far less.

The Pantheon concept penetrated to the outer limits of the Empire. There was once, for example, a domed rotunda, a military trophy or shrine to Victory, in southern Scotland beside the River Carron, dating from the second half of the second century. Known later as Arthur's Oon, it was constructed, by legionaries, of quite carefully cut stone, with a dome fashioned in much the same way as that of the so-called Treasury of Atreus at Mycenae and rising to a height of about twenty-two feet, with a diameter not much less. It was destroyed in the eighteenth century, and nothing seems to be known about the details of its entrance. That it had an oculus is fairly certain.

Round tombs, as we have seen, were common in the Roman world [43–7]. By the middle of the second century, all circular, domed buildings were charged with the imperial concept the Pantheon so eloquently expressed, and the Pantheon idea came to be used for mausolea, especially imperial ones, and also for heroa (shrines for the dead). The round, solid kind of mausoleum built for Augustus and Hadrian [46 and 47] was joined with the Pantheon's powerful imagery of the heavens and the cosmos, and the body of a divinized prince or the spirit of a putative hero was thus housed under a heaven-like vault. With respect to heroa, the ideology was Greek and Hellenistic, the architecture Roman.

One of the earliest domical mausolea, if the second century date assigned to it is correct, once stood in Rome where the sacristy of St Peter's is now [107]. Its original occupant is unknown. In later, Christian times it was known as S. Andrea, still later as S. Maria delle

Febbre; it was demolished in the eighteenth century. Surviving views lead one to conjecture that it was either of a later date or was considerably altered in the fourth century. The large windows in the upper cylinder and the boldly projecting pier-buttresses between them are not, as far as we know, seen in the second century, but rather are features of fourth-century rotunda design. Admittedly the views available may not be entirely accurate. Perhaps the difference between the upper part of the cylinder and the lower part, which does look, with its continuity of surface, like a second-century structure, is the result of fourth-century remodelling or reconstruction; the archaeologists' evidence for dating was chiefly from the lowest portion of the building. It is worth noting these details, because if the views and the second-century date are correct, the disappearance of the exterior seamlessness of the Pantheon rotunda, in favor of the articulation of dome-supporting structures, began earlier than the evidence of a number of other dated monuments seems at present to suggest.

In any event, the domed rotunda, usually but not always with a trabeated porch, became by the year 300 a common form of imperial tomb, copied on a smaller scale by less exalted persons. One additional example may suffice, the so-called Tomb of the Gordians, or Tor de' Schiavi, beside the Via Prenestina leading east from Rome [108 and 109]. Dating from the early fourth century, it bore a close resemblance to the Pantheon, though it had an understorey or crypt, probably for the sarcophagus, a feature common to several grand mausolea of the period (that of Diocletian, 284–305, at Split in Yugoslavia, for example, and the early fourth-century rotunda-tomb, probably built by Maxentius, by the Via Appia outside Rome). Much of the Via Prenestina rotunda stands, fifty Roman feet in interior diameter, and with the same ratio of wall thickness to diameter as the Pantheon, 1 : 7. There was no oculus, the interior being lit by four round windows at the base of the dome. The porch was four-columned and abutted directly onto the rotunda cylinder without an intermediate block. It is possible that an arch stood between the two central façade columns, or even that arches replaced the entablature all around the three sides of the porch. Arches on columns are another distinctive feature of late antique architecture.

By the fourth century, the domed rotunda was well established as a suitable form not only for certain temples and tombs but also for pavilions in palaces and villas. Whereas rotunda tombs tended to be architecturally conservative, the pavilions, in part the descendants of Hadrian's baroque creations at his Villa near Tivoli, were much more advanced, and were at the cutting edge of architectural invention in

107. S. Andrea
by St Peter's, Rome;
view by
M. van Heemskerck.

108. The so-called
Mausoleum of the Gordians,
Rome, early fourth century.

109. The so-called
Mausoleum of the Gordians,
Rome, restored.

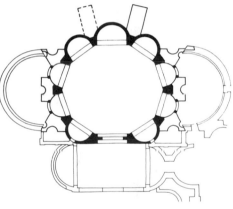

110–13. The so-called
Temple of Minerva Medica, Rome, *c.* 320:
(*top*) view; (*above left*) model;
(*above*) plan; (*left*) detail of dome construction.

their time. The most significant example we have is the so-called Temple of Minerva Medica in Rome, considerable remains of which still stand [110]. This important building, erected just before 320, was a ten-sided structure with a diameter of eighty Roman feet, taken to a circle inscribed in the decagon [111 and 112]. It was pierced by large round-headed windows above, and its interior volume was dilated at ground level by protruding apses on nine of its ten sides (the model shows the building as of 320, as do the solid black areas of the plan, where the single and dotted lines show later additions and alterations, some remains of which can also be seen in the foreground of illustration 110). Of the apses, the two pairs beside the transverse axis were in turn opened up by arcades curving in plan, a major element in later architecture, particularly in the Byzantine style centered in Constantinople. The dome was of the step-ring type [113]. The entranceway, at the only side without an apse, was marked by a high, thin planar wall, rather in the fashion of the wall above the entrance to the so-called Temple of Romulus [106]. There was no porch, the orders being pulled back into the arched recess around the door. The dome was supported on pier-like verticals set between the apses and the windows, and these piers, like the apses, were boldly articulated on the exterior of the building (cf. S. Andrea [107]).

In this kiosk or garden pavilion, probably part of a late imperial palace, the Pantheon appeared in its last major pre-Christian interpretation. The blank rotunda walls had disappeared, not to be seen again until the eighteenth century. The orders were all but eliminated. The structure supporting the dome suggested a skeleton of piers quite clearly stated and, most important, the abstract geometry of the Pantheon's cylinder and sphere had given way to a perforated wall that moved back and forth both inside and out. The Pantheon's enclosed volume had been liberated, and now flowed out to meet and mingle with the space outside the building. Nevertheless it was a Pantheon building, a monumental centralized architectural space domed over, with several Pantheon design elements yet visible, though it is clear that the lines of stylistic connection back to the second century had become rather thin.

EARLY CHRISTIAN [TO c. 450]

The breaking-point came in the Early Christian period, which for our purposes we may regard as a sub-phase of the later imperial age. The temple-front porch, with its uncompromisingly pagan associations, had to go. Centralized single volumetric spaces were not useful to

Christian communities on a grand scale, though they were preserved on a relatively small scale for baptisteries and martyria. Some time before the middle of the fourth century, a radically new idea appeared, which in the simplest terms consisted of placing the cylinder and hemispherical dome of the Pantheon up on piers or columns, stilt-like, and surrounding this entirely with a lower, vaulted ring, an ambulatory or circular aisle. This type, conveniently called the double-shell building, passed into Byzantine architecture where it was used very creatively, the circular plan being abandoned for apsidal, rectangular and polygonal ones; it also had a full life ahead of it in the west.

The key monuments are the Holy Sepulchre in Jerusalem, begun about 330 and later altered almost beyond recognition, and S. Costanza in Rome, probably built about the middle of the century, and very well preserved [114 and 115]. The latter was probably the mausoleum of one of Constantine the Great's family. It is entered through a shallow porch with apsidal ends, and the entranceway is flanked by deep niches. The massive outer, lower wall, shaded on the plan, is divided by niches into the same number of features, sixteen, as the Pantheon. Between this wall and the inner circle of columns is a barrel vault that travels in a ring around the building [116]. The inner shell is composed of pairs of columns, set radially and connected by powerful arches [117], carrying a cylinder and hemispherical dome above. The cylinder and dome reach above the level of the engirdling ring-vault, so that the elevated cylinder can be given windows to light the interior. This puts the outer, human-scaled aisle in relative shade, and illuminates the dome, the symbol of heaven, a good deal more fully. It is rather as if the Minerva Medica had been ringed with a lower, vaulted structure. The origin of the two-shelled building is not certain, but one of its major elements – the domed cylinder of the inner shell – harks back to the Pantheon, as do certain of its details. Yet in it the volumetric unity of the Pantheon had disappeared, not to appear again until the Renaissance.

The double-shell concept can also be seen in certain buildings where the illusion of expanded space was sought, as in the Orthodox Baptistery in Ravenna of about a century after S. Costanza [118]. With the use of brilliantly colored mosaic, partly of glass and gold, and an ingenious interlacing of arcades, the sensation of the presence of working structure was reduced almost to nothing, and the interior culminates in a glittering dome centered over the sacramental font. In buildings such as this, and in the hundreds of buildings that descend from the Holy Sepulchre and S. Costanza, the idea of the heavenly dome was kept viable in the history of architecture. The

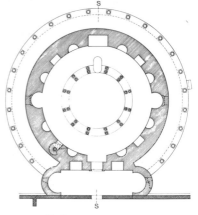

114–17. S. Costanza, Rome, c. 350:
(top) view; (left) interior,
view by Piranesi; (above) plan;
(below left) part of the interior ring-arcade.

118. The Orthodox Baptistery, Ravenna, interior, c. 400–450.

change in the Pantheon's dedication about 609 from all gods to all
martyr saints paralleled exactly the ready shift in meaning, during the
early middle ages, of its architectural imagery.

Meanwhile Rome had shriveled, physically and above all creatively.
It was no longer a city of consequence except as a legendary symbol.
Architectural creativity had moved east, to Constantinople, and north,

to Lombardy and beyond, to places where art took new and different forms. Laments sung over the city conjure up a desolation:

> Rome, once the head of the world, the world's pride, the city of gold,
> Stands now a pitiful ruin, the wreck of its glory of old.

So the scholar Alcuin, in the time of Charlemagne. During the next six centuries, Roman ideas in architecture were ever more diluted, until they disappeared almost entirely. Byzantine architecture, in the east, and Gothic, in the west, replaced them.

But Rome itself did not die, though sacked, and abandoned by all authority. As early as the twelfth century there were signs of attention to the antiquities of the city as well as to its pagan institutions. In 1143 a Senate was proclaimed on the Capitol, and a few years later the first version of a pilgrims' guide to the city appeared, the *Mirabilia Romae*. One-third fact, two-thirds pious legend, the *Mirabilia* persisted well into the age of printing, accompanied by illustrations of the city's marvels which, judging from late versions and related picture plans of the city, showed the Pantheon in a crudely simple way [119]. Thus, before the age of humanism was well under way, some of the great monuments surviving from the distant past could be known, at least in a vague fashion, through manuscript descriptions, simple illustrations, and picture maps [120 and 121].

THE RENAISSANCE
(FIFTEENTH AND EARLY SIXTEENTH CENTURIES)

Humanist enquiry, and the desire of the popes to make Rome a monumental capital again, brought about the second, Renaissance phase of the history we are pursuing. The humanists believed that knowledge of the past, so highly valued and so passionately desired, could be gained rationally. In architecture, this stimulated an immense amount of observation and measuring of ancient buildings; naturally the Pantheon was a major subject. Of the many Renaissance drawings of the building, few are more elegant or accurate than a longitudinal section by Peruzzi (1481–1536) of the early 1530s [122]. The building is observed scientifically; the drawing is to scale, with its main lines laid out with instruments, and key elements of structure and decoration are included. Even the slight crowning of the rotunda pavement is recorded.

In theory, Vitruvius' text was the Renaissance architect's bible, but in practice his influence, though great, was not as all-pervasive as the literature of the time might seem to suggest. He was studied

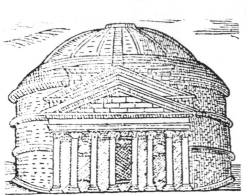

119. The Pantheon from *Mirabilia Urbis Romae*.

120 (*right*). Detail from
The Departure of St Augustine from Rome,
by Gozzoli, 1465.

121 (*below*). View of Rome, 1490.

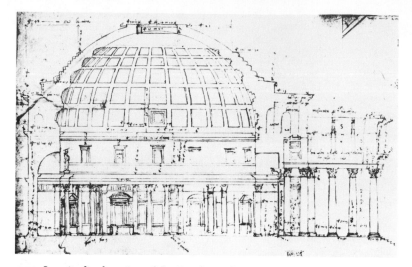

122. Longitudinal section of the Pantheon, by Peruzzi, *c.* 1530–40.

assiduously, and in any disagreement he was sure to be cited extensively. But the architecture of which he wrote, in the time of Augustus and Agrippa, was on the whole not the ancient architecture the Renaissance knew so well, the architecture of imperial Rome, particularly of the second, third, and early fourth centuries. Moreover, in his own day Vitruvius was rather conservative, and there is no mention in his writings of the grand, innovative architectural compositions of the later Republic – monuments he could not possibly have failed to know, such as the huge sanctuaries at Palestrina and Tivoli – that so attracted Renaissance architects. In design, his influence was greatest with respect to the orders, for his rules for their proportions and dispositions were regarded as sacrosanct. His technical advice remained on the whole sound, for little had changed with regard to methods of construction and materials. His proud advertisement of the dignity and usefulness of the profession of architecture, and his ample list of the disciplines to be mastered by anyone who would succeed at it, fitted humanist ideals exactly. But the divergence between the architecture of his own time and the monuments the Renaissance most admired cannot be ignored. Vitruvius is not much help in the study of the Pantheon, except with regard to some details of the porch trabeation, and the background of the rotunda's proportions.

The example of antiquity was not to be followed mindlessly, but was to be looked upon as a source of inspiration. Ancient architecture, from the early fifteenth century on, was seen also as a challenge, for what for the most part was a confident age sought to emulate the grandeur and scale of the monuments of the past. For the first time in a thousand years the monuments began to get the kind of professional attention they so badly needed. In 1515, pope Leo X made Raphael his Superintendent of Antiquities and subsequently he, probably with the help of others more accustomed to writing government documents, made a report to the pope on the condition of the monuments, the need to measure them accurately and in detail, and the possibilities of successful restoration.

A passage from a widely-read treatise by the architect Sebastiano Serlio (1475–1554), published in sections between 1537 and 1551, gives a sense of the attitudes of the times. He is leading up to detailed, practical architectural information about the Pantheon, for, like Vitruvius, Serlio tended to emphasize structure and methods of building.

> Among all the ancient buildings to be seen in Rome, I am of the opinion that the Pantheon . . . is the fairest, the most whole, and the best to be understood. It is so much more wonderful than the rest because it has so many members which are all correspondent one to the other, so that whoever looks at it takes great pleasure in it. This is because the excellent architect who devised it chose the purest form, that is the round form, from which it is usually called S. Mary of the Rotunda ; within it is as high as it is broad . . . the Pantheon seems to me to be the most perfect piece of work I ever saw . . . the measures of all the members are as well observed as I ever saw or measured in any other piece of work . . . I will proceed to give its particular dimensions . . .

Renaissance principles allowed antiquity to be fully exploited. The temple front, for example, reappeared. Circular buildings were in a sense rediscovered, for all great Renaissance and Baroque architects studied the probems connected with the composition and construction of centralized buildings. Architecture had rules, or *regole*, and it was believed that the proper understanding of these would prevent failure; antiquity was the school in which the regole were to be learned. And where could they be learned better than at the Pantheon, both the temple of all gods and the church of all martyr saints, where the ancient canopy of the heavens had been marvelously preserved and had come to symbolize the unified and perfect justice of God.

As early as 1444, Michelozzo had 'copied' the so-called Temple of Minerva Medica [110–13], in the centralized addition he built for the medieval church of the Annunziata in Florence. When in 1506 the rebuilding of St Peter's in Rome was given by Julius II to Bramante, the plan he proposed was that of the arms of a cross inscribed in an immense square. The four ends of the cross ended in huge Roman apses that projected from the girdling walls [123]. At the center of the whole, where the arms crossed, Bramante proposed to raise the equivalent of the dome of the Pantheon [124], and such was the cultural climate of the time that this was found not only acceptable but admirable: the legendary symbol of pagan Rome could properly adorn the new church of churches. And when, later in the century, Michelangelo took over the vast uncompleted building, he proposed that an enormous temple-front porch be added. Behind this temple-front, never built, the plane of Michelangelo's attic (an attic that ran around the entire building masking and stabilizing the lower part of the apse vaults and the barrel vaults of the cross arms) would, with the colossal pediment in front of it, have emphasized the church's connection with the Pantheon. But the silhouette of the Pantheon dome was too flat for the exterior effect the new St Peter's required; Bramante's Pantheon-like dome was abandoned and in its place, in due course, the present higher vault was built. Even so, the very concept of a dome, of the meanings inherent in domical symbolism (in this case over the traditional martyr shrine of the first of the apostles) was of ancient origin, and the ideological and historical connections with antiquity would not go unnoticed. The idea and symbols of Rome, *The* City, were very potent in the cultivated Roman Renaissance mind.

ANDREA PALLADIO (1508–80)

The third phase centers around the work of one man, 'the most imitated architect in history'. Palladio was a professional of great and original talent, a learned man, author, and antiquarian. In his work, the ardent Renaissance study of ancient buildings reached perhaps its most complete expression. But he, as much as any other architect who knew ancient architecture intimately, was a man of the regole, a maker of systems of design and a slave to symmetry. His buildings – nearly fifty villas, palaces, civic structures, and churches, all in northern Italy – never copy antiquity and, although he studied Vitruvius thoroughly, he used the Vitruvian rules only when they suited him. He spent several years in Rome during the 1540s and 1550s and made many drawings of the ancient monuments. In 1550 an edition of Vitruvius was published with his illustrations; he collaborated to some degree in the preparation of the text. Four years later he published two books of his own, one on the antiquities of Rome and the other on its churches,

123. Design for St Peter's,
bronze coin by
Cristoforo Caradosso, 1506.

124. Design for
the dome of St Peter's.

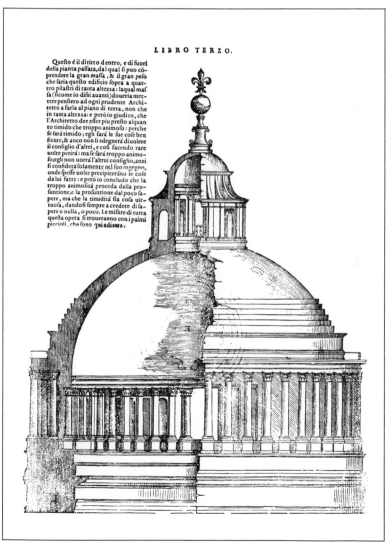

LIBRO TERZO.

Questo è il diritto d'entro, e di fuori della pianta paſſata, dal qual ſi puo cóprendere la gran maſſa, & il gran peſo che ſaria queſto edificio ſopra a quattro pilaſtri di tanta altezza: laqual maſſa (ſicome io diſſi auanti)doueria mettere penſiero ad ogni prudente Architetto a farla al piano di terra, non che in tanta altezza: e peró io giudico, che l'Architetto dee eſſer piu preſto alquanto timido che troppo animoſo: perche ſe ſarà timido; egli farà le ſue coſe ben ſicure, & anco nón ſi ſdegnerà di uolere il conſiglio d'altri, e coſi facendo rare uolte perirà: ma ſe ſarà troppo animoſo; egli non uorrà l'altrui conſiglio, anzi ſi conſiderà ſolamente nel ſuo ingegno, onde ſpeſſe uolte precipiteráno le coſe da lui fatte: e peró io concludo che la troppo animoſità proceda dalla proſuntione, e la proſuntione dal poco ſapere, ma che la timidità ſia coſa uirtuoſa, dandoſi ſempre a credere di ſapere o nulla, o poco. Le miſure di tutta queſta opera ſi troueranno con i palmi piccioli, che ſono qui adioſſo.

and in 1570 his *Quattro libri dell'architettura* appeared, one of the most influential architectural books ever written. In it, theory was subordinated to practice, and the text was supplemented by many of his drawings of his own work and of ancient Roman buildings. The regole, particularly with respect to the orders, are there in force. In 1730 Lord Burlington published Palladio's drawings of Roman baths, and in recent times his life and work have been studied in detail. In his architecture there are many designs and projects inspired by or related to the Pantheon, while his drawings of antiquities include many of the Pantheon itself [125] and of ruins he restored with Pantheon-like structures. His books, and the work of his disciples, particularly Lord Burlington, gave him the status of a second Vitruvius, and through him knowledge of the Pantheon spread far and wide.

At his famous Villa Rotonda near Vicenza, of 1550, a Pantheon-like step-ring dome rises from a cylindrical room encased in a cubical block [126]. From the block project four grand temple-front porches, carried on monumental podia; the attics behind the porch pediments recall the Pantheon. At Maser in 1579–80, at the end of his life, he built a delightful chapel that has been called an 'irreverent child of the Pantheon' [127 and 128]. The porch was reduced from eight columns to six, and the building is high for its width. Twin towers appear, and it can be seen from the plan that the apsidal and transverse niches extend outside the rotunda periphery in a manner recalling the Round Temple at Ostia. The dome supports are cleverly integrated with the niche extensions. By comparison the Pantheon appears sombre, but it should always be recalled that the Pantheon's proportions have been much altered by the considerable rise of ground around it; greater height would give it a somewhat lighter and less forbiddingly massive presence. The chapel at Maser is almost frivolous in appearance, an impression due as much as anything to the sculptured swags that depend from the porch capitals. It has gaiety and verges on the Rococo. None of this, however, disguises its obvious ancestry, and it is the nearest thing to a copy of the Pantheon since the Temple of Asklepios at Pergamon or the Tor de' Schiavi.

The addition of twin towers is important. As we have seen, the Pantheon was given a set forty-five years afterwards which stood for two and a half centuries [14]. That new arrangement of the Pantheon's façade was an important element in the evolution of classicizing architecture from the early seventeenth century onward. Present opinion is that the Maser chapel, tucked away in a village in the central Veneto, was probably unknown to architects working in Rome – Palladio did not illustrate it in the *Quattro libri* – and the source

125. The Pantheon, from A. Palladio's *Four Books on Architecture.*

126. Villa Rotonda, Vicenza, by Palladio, 1550.

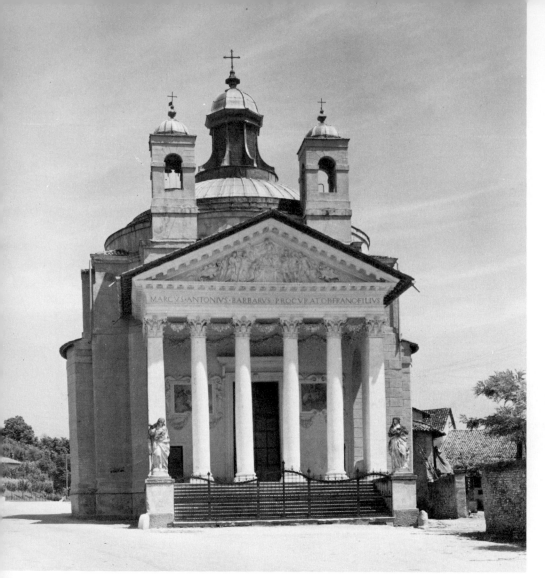

127 and 128. The chapel,
Maser, by Palladio, 1579–80:
view and plan.

of the Pantheon's towers must be sought elsewhere. But the exclusion of Maser is really guesswork; there are apparently no relevant documents. There is, however, other evidence. In Rome, the church of S. Atanasio dei Greci was given a twin-tower façade in the early 1580s, the work of Giacomo della Porta, while Vignola, a contemporary of Palladio's who worked in Rome, had proposed one for the church of the Gesù in the 1560s. Before that, twin towers had been planned by Bramante and Sangallo for the new St Peter's. These and similar developments could answer the question of the immediate sources of the Pantheon's towers. But as Palladio's Maser design seems to have been the first such design actually built, and as Palladio studied the Pantheon with great care during his Roman sojourns, it may be productive to ask what he could see that has since disappeared.

In 1616, in Rome, a book of views of the antiquities of Rome was published by Alò Giovannoli (c. 1550–1618). In it was the plate showing the Pantheon [10] to which we referred when discussing the appearance of the building prior to the restorations and changes made for Urban VIII in the 1620s and 1630s. Giovannoli shows the thirteenth-century bell tower still standing and, on either side of it, dwarfish towers abutting an intermediate block whose bounding horizontal cornice is much abbreviated. There are palpable errors in the view, such as the displacement of the left-hand or east niche of the intermediate block, but the towers, which may have been simply hoods for the staircase exits, are not likely to have been gratuitous inventions by Giovannoli and it may be that it was from them that the twin-tower façade idea descended. In any event, the Giovannoli view probably shows, in a general way, what Palladio saw. Palladio, of course, studied this part of the Pantheon very carefully, and he made much use of it in his own buildings and projects, for example when he placed a pediment on the front of a façade wall of rectangular outline. In his day the Pantheon's second, upper pediment had not been restored as one sees it today, but was divided into two parts by the bell tower; its upper angle had disappeared [cf. 9]. This effect Palladio adapted brilliantly to his own architecture by taking the two slanting, truncated cornices and placing them on the flanks of the central temple-fronts of his great Venetian church façades [129].

THE SEVENTEENTH CENTURY

By the turn of the century, books by Serlio, Palladio, and others were widely available in Europe. Foreign architects or aspirants had appeared in Rome in the sixteenth century, and the number grew

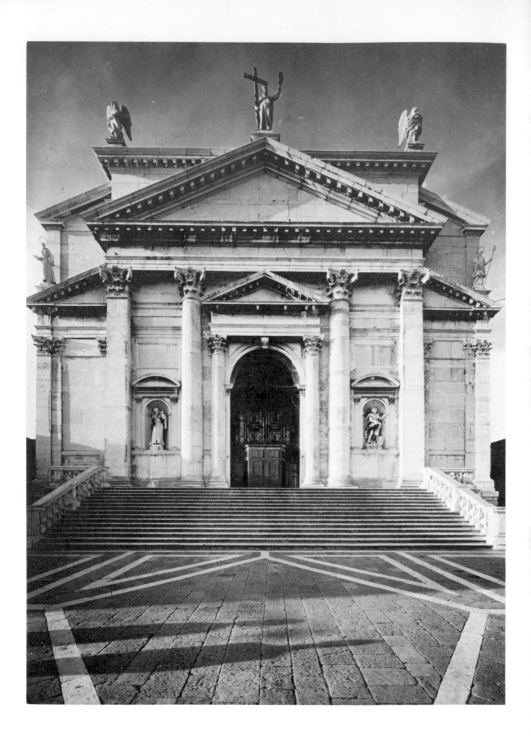

129. Il Redentore, Venice, by Palladio, begun 1576.

considerably in the seventeenth, when a prolonged stay in Rome became almost obligatory for anyone who would pursue architecture correctly. In 1666 the French Academy was founded there, the first of a number of foreign establishments for the study of art and architecture. And all serious visitors sketched, measured, and even on occasion excavated antiquities. The Rome these foreigners saw was that of the Counter Reformation, the contemporary art Baroque [83], but the Roman architects of the seventeenth century were in their own way as devoted to antiquity as their predecessors, and just as unable to ignore their surroundings and their heritage. Thus the history of the idea and influence of the Pantheon continued in the Baroque age, not least because the rejuvenated papacy required that the majesty of the ancient city be closely associated with the Church. It was typical of the age that the broken Pantheon porch was now at last repaired, for the building's history and symbolism exactly fitted the principles of continuity and reaffirmed universality upon which the Counter Reformation Church rested. Typical also was the proliferation of domed churches with temple-front façades, as for example the two handsome guardians that stand in the Piazza del Popolo [130] at the north entrance to the city, S. Maria di Montèsanto, left, and S. Maria dei Miracoli.

Two churches by Gianlorenzo Bernini (1598–1680) record the continuing interest in the Pantheon. S. Andrea al Quirinale in Rome, of 1658–70, is a brilliant re-interpretation of the Pantheon's principles in a free adaptation. The church is close to the street and its entrance-way, like that of the so-called Temple of Romulus in the forum, is focused at the back of a shallow incurving court [131; cf. 106]. The entranceway proper is a reduction of the temple-front concept to a pediment supported on tall pilaster-piers (rows of free-standing columns evenly spaced were utterly antithetical to Baroque architectural principles). From this frame a part of a small tholos projects, and the difference in scale between this and the enframing pilasters and pediments gives the little church considerable monumentality. Behind is a single volume, oval in plan and transverse to the axis of the entrance [132]. Ten deep niches – including the entrance bay and apse – are set around the oval, and the apse, as at the Pantheon, is guarded by free-standing columns [cf. 81].

At Ariccia, not far outside Rome to the southeast, Bernini built the church of S. Maria dell'Assunzione in 1662–4 [133]. Here his close study of the Pantheon – a number of his drawings of it exist – was put to use even more directly. The portico is composed of arches and piers, and while there is no intermediate block, the cylindrical body of the

130. Piazza del Popolo, Rome,
view by Piranesi, 1756.

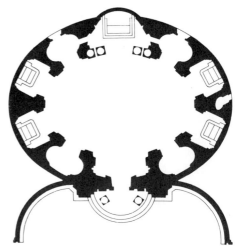

131 and 132. S. Andrea al Quirinale, Rome,
by Bernini, 1658–70: view and plan.

133 and 134.
S. Maria dell'Assunzione,
Ariccia, by Bernini, 1662–4:
view and plan.

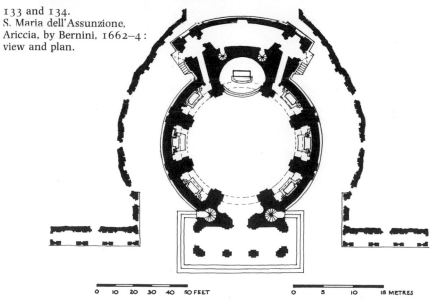

0 10 20 30 40 50 FEET   0   5   10   15 METRES

135. The bagno
at Chiswick,
by Lord Burlington, 1717.

136. The Pantheon
at Stourhead, 1753–4.

137. The Pantheon.
London, by James Wyatt,
1770–72.

rotunda is clearly taken from the Pantheon, though it is much smaller, about sixty feet in interior diameter [134]. There are six niches, an apse, and an entrance bay, and therefore eight piers; there are twin towers, but they are placed at the back of the rotunda. Bernini, a man of extraordinary talents, was the artist most representative of the Italian Baroque, and his regard for the Pantheon and use of it is impressive evidence of its continuing potency. In seeking to comprehend its original appearance, he seems to have envisaged it in Augustan times (for so the Agrippan inscription dated it), free from all decorative intrusions, which he took to be later work; the Ariccia church reflects his convictions. He remarked that the dome of St Peter's was beautiful, unequaled in antiquity, but that it had a hundred faults, while the Pantheon had none.

NEO-CLASSIC

(EIGHTEENTH AND EARLY NINETEENTH CENTURIES)

During the last two phases, the Neo-Classic and modern, the domed rotunda with a temple-front façade became common in all western architecture. In 1682, accurate measured drawings of the Pantheon were published by Antoine Desgodetz (1653–1728), who was sent to Rome from Paris with the specific assignment of measuring certain ancient buildings. This he did extremely conscientiously. His published work was several times reprinted and was translated into English toward the end of the eighteenth century. But many architects went to see for themselves, though now there were more gentlemen amateurs, some of them very gifted, than professionals, for the Grand Tour was at full tide. Englishmen were particularly in evidence, the noblemen often with an architect or a would-be architect in tow, in the fashion of Inigo Jones's attendance upon Lord Arundel in Rome during the previous century. By the middle of the eighteenth century, classical art began to oust the Rococo, and in the second half of the century the fervor for things antique was boundless. In this atmosphere the Pantheon idea flourished.

As early as 1717, Lord Burlington designed a Pantheon, called a bagno, for the park of his estate at Chiswick near London [135]. Palladio inspired it, for Palladio was Burlington's passion; later he was to make an extensive collection of Palladio's drawings, and it will be recalled that in 1730 he published the invaluable drawings of the ruins of the imperial baths or thermae of Rome. The regole had found a home in England. Pantheons, and round buildings on the model of of classical tholoi with Pantheon domes, as at Stowe and Stourhead

[136], built in 1743–4, sprang up all over England as Palladianism became for most the only proper architectural style. Imitators thrived. Pope, in a charming address to Burlington about architecture, observed that

> Conscious they act a true Palladian part,
> And, if they starve, they starve by rules of art.

Less derivative architects used classical architecture more freely. James Wyatt (1747–1813), for example, in his Pantheon in London of 1770–72, placed the form of a coffered dome some fifty feet in diameter over a plan of a distinctly Byzantine kind [137]. It was an immense success and made Wyatt's name.

The Pantheon idea generated similar excitement in other countries. Frederick the Great helped Knobelsdorff add an elegant domed rotunda to Sans Souci at Potsdam, and in Berlin in the 1750s Legeay built the Hedwigskirche in the form of a Pantheon with a shallow Ionic porch [138]. In Karlsruhe Weinbrenner, who had studied in Rome, designed a Catholic Church in the manner of the Pantheon, which was built in 1808–17; it was radically altered in the 1880s.

In Paris, Soufflot's Sainte-Geneviève, now called the Panthéon, was begun in 1757; it owes little if anything to the Roman Pantheon apart from its name, which it acquired when secularized during the Revolution. However, it was in France that the Pantheon was to find the most fervent and radical of all its interpreters, beginning with Gondouin, whose anatomy theatre of 1765–75 at the École de Médecine in Paris is an exact half-Pantheon [139] – a half cylinder covered by a quarter-sphere – and continuing into the Revolutionary years with Boullée whose design of c. 1780 for the Paris Opéra was a half-Pantheon within a sphere [140]. Even more extreme were Vaudoyer and Le Queux in designs such as those for a 'Maison d'un Cosmopolite' and for a temple to 'La Sagesse Suprême' [141] of 1785 and 1794 respectively. The spherical basis of the Pantheon's design attracted these revolutionary architects, who aspired to an architecture of pure form. Indeed, they went further than their prototype and actually gave their Pantheon-inspired designs a spherical form internally – and sometimes externally as well. Not surprisingly, few were ever built.

However, this radical current of French late-eighteenth-century architecture did eventually find expression in actual buildings, for example in Bélanger's remarkable cast iron spherical dome for the Halle au Blé in Paris of 1808–13 [142] and, outside France, in Decimus

Burton's so-called Colosseum of 1823–7, in Regent's Park in London. This housed a vast spherical panorama, the interior viewing terrace of which could, if one chose, be reached by a form of primitive lift, raised by manpower [143]. Other examples are Schinkel's central Pantheon hall of the Berlin Altes Museum of 1824–8, and Smirke's Reading Room of the British Museum, London, 1848–56, whose first design, later modified, was spherically proportioned. Some years earlier than either of these, and probably directly inspired by Boullée, is Jefferson's great library rotunda at the University of Virginia of 1817–26 with, once again, a spherically proportioned interior [144].

In Italy, the examples stretch from S. Simeone Piccolo in Venice [145], by Scalfarotto, of about 1718–30, to the Gran'Madre di Dio in Turin, by Bonsignore, of 1818–31, and S. Carlo al Corso in Milan, [146], by Amati, of 1836–47. The austere, linear qualities that Neo-Classic design could project are seen in S. Francesco di Paolo in Naples, by Bianchi, built in 1817–46 [147]. The flanking curved colonnades are of slightly earlier date, part of a semi-elliptical piazza into which the church was introduced for King Ferdinand I. Inside the building Pliny's caryatids appear once more, metamorphosed into angels [148].

At Possagno in the Veneto, six or eight miles northwest of Maser, there is a parish church designed by Canova, the great Neo-Classic sculptor, in the form of a Pantheon rotunda about ninety feet high [149]. With a severe Doric façade and a low pediment reminiscent of the Athenian Parthenon, the Tempio di Canova combines Greek and Roman architecture with startling results. The noisy clash of the two styles is a telling antidote to the common error of treating them simply as divisions of a single architectural period. The building was begun in 1819 and finished in 1833, after Canova's death. With the application of the Pantheon type to mausolea – and this was common in the Neo-Classic period – a basic idea had come full circle, a reversion to the usage of late imperial times. The Panthéon in Paris, for example, was projected as a burial place for heroes of the Revolution. In the United States Capitol in Washington, below the crypt of the central rotunda, there remains an empty sepulchral chamber intended to take the bodies of George and Martha Washington. Above, since 1865, in the rotunda proper, presidents and other national figures have lain in state.

In a related development, the idea spread widely that a Pantheon was a shrine for national worthies where their effigies would be displayed; it seems to have originated in northern Europe. By 1776 busts of famous men, especially men connected with the arts, began

138. The Hedwigskirche, Berlin, by Legeay, 1747.

139. The Anatomy Theater, Paris, by Gondouin, 1765–75.

140. Design for the Opéra, Paris, by Boullée, *c.* 1780.

141. Design by
J. J. Le Queux, 1794.

142. Halle au Blé, Paris,
by F. J. Bélanger, 1808–13.

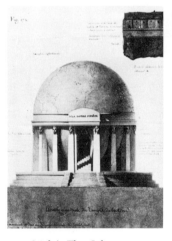

143 (*right*). The Colosseum,
Regent's Park, London,
by Decimus Burton, 1823–34.

144. The Library Rotunda,
University of Virginia,
by Jefferson, 1817–26.

145. S. Simeone Piccolo,
Venice, by Scalfarotto,
c. 1718–30.

146. S. Carlo al Corso, Milan, by Amati, 1836–47.

147. S. Francesco di Paola,
Naples, by Bianchi, 1817–46.

148. S. Francesco di Paola, interior.

149. The Tempio, Possagno, by Canova, 1819–33.

150. St Mary, Mosta, Malta,
by Grognet de Vassé, 1833–60.

151. Dome of St Mary, Mosta.

152. Monticello, Charlottesville,
by Jefferson, begun 1809.

153. The Church of the Immaculate Heart
of Mary, Rome, by M. Piacentini, 1950–60.

154. The Church of Divine Wisdom, Rome,
by M. Piacentini, 1948.

to be placed in the Pantheon in Rome. In the Capitol in Washington there is a Hall of Statuary, formerly the House of Representatives, a room of the half-Pantheon type, next to the central rotunda, that contains images of famous men from the several states.

AFTER 1830

The austerity of the Neo-Classic interpretations of the Pantheon gave way, after about 1830, to versions whose distance from the original depend on the influence of the various historical styles recapitulated in the Victorian era. At Mosta on the island of Malta, for example, the stone-domed church of St Mary, designed by Grognet de Vassé and built in 1833–60, is typical of the eclectic approach of the times [150]. The temple front is continued across the tower bases, Greek ornament appears in and above the pediment and on the drum, and the bell towers are pastiches of various styles. The dome, however, is an engineering triumph, one of the largest masonry vaults in the world [151].

The Pantheon motif can be seen wherever authority, ecclesiastical or political, demanded a recognizable, stately architectural imagery. The evidence of the multiplication in the nineteenth and twentieth centuries of churches, civic and academic buildings, libraries, and capitols, inspired directly or indirectly by the Pantheon, is manifest. In the United States, many such buildings descend directly from Jefferson's Monticello, begun in 1809 [152], and his library rotunda at the University of Virginia, mentioned above. Nearly every past architectural style has been resurrected in modern times, and most have been applied to the Pantheon concept. The diversity produced is suggested by two of Piacentini's buildings in Rome, the Church of the Immaculate Heart of Mary, of the 1950s, in a muscular neo-Baroque manner [153], and the Church of Divine Wisdom, given in 1948 by Pius XII to the University, an exercise in stripped-down classicism [154].

Why did the Pantheon idea persist so long? In historical terms the Renaissance is mainly responsible, for in its return to antiquity the rotunda concept was reborn. The Pantheon, from being thought an awesome wonder, one of the *mirabilia*, became a building seen as designed and constructed not by demons but by men, to be studied and utilized. Because it is in Rome, it has always been quite accessible; one can suggest the significance of this fact by asking what might have happened in architecture if the Parthenon or the Hagia Sophia had stood as intact and accessible to Renaissance and later architects.

Symbolically and ideologically the Pantheon idea survived because it describes satisfactorily, in architectural form, something close to the core of human needs and aspirations. By abstracting the shape of the earth and the imagined form of the cosmos into a grand, immediately assimilated image, the architect of the Pantheon gave mankind a symbol that transcends religion, class, and political conviction. In contrast to Gothic architecture, for example, the Pantheon's religious associations are ambiguous, if they exist at all. Because it was not freighted with any sectarian or localized meaning, and because of the universality inherent in its forms, it was unendingly adaptable. It is one of the very few archetypal images in western architecture.

The temple-fronted, domed rotunda persisted also because it was adopted by authority both despotic and democratic, for which it was extremely suitable for several reasons. It is a monumental form, on any scale, because of its bold and simple geometry. It is entirely free of the architectural characteristics of domestic or commercial buildings, and there is not a hint in it of the individual or the idiosyncratic; it has surpassing dignity. A Pantheon-like building also expresses a permanence solidly based, due partly to its powerful symmetry and the hierarchy of forms that rise from the podium up through the pediment to the crown of the dome; partly to its incorporation, in the temple-front, of the most expressive and readily recognized symbol of that Mediterranean cultural heritage, woven through with law and principles of government, common to all western peoples. But most of all, permanence is expressed by the centered dome, the shape most suggestive of fixed and immutable rules because its unbroken, encircling sphericity evokes the stability of the firmament itself. The very word rotunda, common to several languages, has a ring of permanence and solidity.

Entered through a porch built up from bold forms — powerful columns carrying the most stable of geometric figures, the broad-based triangle — a domed rotunda is a place where one can partake, symbolically, of the immutable laws and hoped-for tranquillity of the universe. There the lower order is united with the higher, the unity of which Hadrian dreamed. A Pantheon is neither sacred nor secular, but a place of man and nature, of man and the forces the ancients called the gods.

Future investigations may possibly show
that Roman architecture was not as dull as it now appears.
I fear, however, that this is unlikely.
A. K. Porter, 1919

Disegno angelico e non umano.
Michelangelo

BIBLIOGRAPHY

ANCIENT SOURCES

Ammianus Marcellinus, conveniently available in the Loeb Classical Library, a collection of Greek and Latin texts with English translations, London, and Cambridge Mass.

Codex Theodosianus, ed. T. Mommsen and P. M. Meyer, 2 vols., Berlin, 1905; English translation by C. Pharr, Princeton, 1952.

Dio Cassius, also in the Loeb collection.

The Marble Plan of Rome (*Forma Urbis Romae*): G. Carretoni and others, *La pianta marmorea di Roma antica*, 2 vols., Rome, 1960. The plan was made about A.D. 200.

Pliny the Elder, *Natural History*, also in the Loeb collection.

Scriptores Historiae Augustae, biographies of the emperors from Hadrian onward; mixtures of fact and fiction; also in the Loeb collection.

Vitruvius (probably Marcus Vitruvius Pollio), *Ten Books on Architecture*. Available in the Loeb collection, but there is a better English translation by M. H. Morgan, Cambridge, Mass., 1914, paperback edition New York, 1960; both versions are illustrated. See also F. E. Brown, below.

MODERN WORKS

Armellini, M., *Le chiese di Roma del secolo IV al XIX*, 3rd edition, 2 vols., Rome, 1942.

Bartoccetti, V., *Santa Maria ad Martyres (Pantheon)*, Rome, 1959 (a guidebook).

Beltrami, L., *Il Pantheon*, Milan, 1898, and *Il Pantheon rivendicato ad Adriano*, Milan, 1929.

Bettini, S., *L'architettura di San Marco (origini e significato)*, Padua, 1946, pp. 85–127 and 149–91.

Blake, M. E., *Ancient Roman Construction in Italy . . . to Augustus*, Washington D.C., 1947; *Roman Construction in Italy from Tiberius through the Flavians*, Washington D.C., 1959, and *Roman Construction in Italy from Nerva through the Antonines*, ed. and completed by D. T. Bishop, Philadelphia, 1973.

Boëthius, A., and J.B. Ward-Perkins, *Etruscan and Roman Architecture*, Penguin Books, 1970 (the best handbook).

Brown, F.C. and others, *A Study of the Orders*, revised by J.R. Dalzell, Chicago, 1948.

Brown, F.E., *Roman Architecture*, New York, 1961 (excellent brief survey), and 'Vitruvius and the Liberal Act of Architecture', *Bucknell Review*, 11.4, 1963, pp. 99–107.

Cerasoli, F., 'I restauri del Pantheon dal secolo XV al XVIII', *Bulletino della commissione archeologica communale di Roma*, 37, 1909, pp. 280–89.

Colini, A.M., and I. Gismondi, 'Contributi allo studio del Pantheon', *Bulletino della commissione archeologica communale di Roma*, 54, 1926 (pub. 1927), pp. 67–92.

Colonna, G.B., 'Il Pantheon', *Capitolium*, 14, 1934, pp. 240–49.

Crema, L., *L'architettura romana*, Turin, 1959 (=*Enciclopedia classica* 3.12.1; handbook, detailed), and 'Il pronao del Pantheon', *Collection Latomus* 58, 1962, pp. 457–61 (=*Hommages à A. Grenier*, I).

Desgodetz, A., *Les Édifices antiques de Rome*, 2nd edition, Paris, 1779, pp. 1–26 and Plates I–XXIII (original edition 1682; Desgodetz' foot = 0·325 m.); cf. *Art Bulletin*, 40, 1958, pp. 23–4.

Durm, J., *Die Baukunst der Etrusker: Die Baukunst der Römer*, 2nd edition, Stuttgart, 1905.

Egger, H., *Römische Veduten*, 2 vols., Vienna, 1911–31.

Eroli, G.M., *Raccolta generale delle inscrizioni pagane e cristiane esistite ed esistente nel Pantheon di Roma*, Narni, 1895.

D'Espouy, H., *Fragments d'architecture antique*, 2 vols., Paris, 1896–1905, and *Monuments antiques relevés et restaurés par les architects pensionnaires de l'Académie de France à Rome*, 3 vols., Paris, 1906, supplementary vol. 1923 (the Pantheon drawings of A. Leclère are in vol. 2).

de Fine Licht, K., *The Rotunda in Rome: A Study of Hadrian's Pantheon*, Copenhägen, 1968 (=*Jutland Archeological Society*, 8; detailed and fully documented).

de Geymuller, H., *Documents inédits sur les Thermes d'Agrippa, le Panthéon et les Thermes de Dioclétian*, Lausanne and Rome, 1883.

Giovannoni, G., *La tecnica della costruzione presso i romani*, Rome, 1925; 'Pantheon', *Architettura et arti decorative*, 8, 1928–9, pp. 526–8; and 'Building and Engineering', in *The Legacy of Ancient Rome*, ed. C. Bailey, Oxford, 1951, pp. 429–74.

Gullini, G., *Il problema dello spazio nell'architettura greca e romana*, Turin, 1958.

Hirt, L., *Osservazioni istorico-architettoniche sopra il Pantheon*, Rome, 1791.

Kähler, H., *Hadrian und seine Villa bei Tivoli*, Berlin, 1950 (Hadrian and architecture); 'Das Pantheon in Rom', in *Meilensteine europäischer Kunst*, ed. E. Steingräber, Munich, 1965, pp. 47–75 and 429–31, and 'The Pantheon as Sacral Art', *Bucknell Review*, 15.2, 1967, pp. 41–8.

Kaschnitz von Weinberg, G., *Die Baukunst im Kaiserreich*, Hamburg, 1963 (brief, good survey).

Lanciani, R., *Ruins and Excavations of Ancient Rome*, London, Boston and New York, 1897 (pagination differs slightly); 'Prima relazione sugli scavi per lo isolamento del Pantheon', *Notizie degli scavi di antichità*, 1881, pp. 255–94, and 'Seconda relazione . . .', 1882, pp. 340–59.

Lugli, G., *La tecnica edilizia romana*, 2 vols., Rome, 1957, reprinted New York and London, 1968.

MacDonald, W. L., *The Architecture of the Roman Empire, I: An Introductory Study*, New Haven, 1965.

Montani, C., 'Il Pantheon e i suoi recenti restauri', *Capitolium*, 8, 1932, pp. 417–26.

Nash, E., *Pictorial Dictionary of Ancient Rome*, revised edition, 2 vols., London, 1968 (invaluable, full biographies).

D'Ossat, G. de Angelis, 'La forma e la costruzione delle cupole nell'architettura romana', *Atti del III convegno nazionale di storia dell'architettura*, 1938, published 1940, pp. 223–50 (= *Saggi sull'architettura etrusca e romana*).

Rivoira, G. T., *Roman Architecture and its Principles of Construction under the Empire*, trans. G. McN. Rushforth, Oxford, 1925, reprinted 1972; original Italian edition, Milan 1921; and 'Di Adriano architetto e dei monumenti adrianei', *Rendiconti dell'Accademia nazionale dei Lincei*, 18, 1909, pp. 172–7.

Rodocanachi, E., 'Le Panthéon', *La Revue de l'art ancien et moderne*, 34, 1913, pp. 279–86 and 365–76.

Sanguinetti, F., 'Nota sul consolidamento della trabeazione del pronao del Pantheon', *Palladio*, 6, 1956, pp. 78–9.

Terenzio, A., 'La Restauration du Panthéon de Rome', *Museion*, 20, pp. 52–7, and 'Pantheon', *Enciclopedia italiana*, 26, 1935, pp. 212–14.

Tomei, P., 'Le vicende del rivistimento della cupola del Pantheon', *Bolletino d'arte*, 32, 1938, pp. 31–9.

Vighi, R., *The Pantheon*, trans. J. B. Ward-Perkins, Rome, 1957 (a guidebook; there are editions in other languages).

Von Gerkan, 'Das Pantheon in Rom', *Gnomon*, 5, 1929, pp. 273–7.

Yourcenar, M., *Hadrian's Memoirs*, New York, 1957; originally *Mémoires d'Hadrien*, Paris, 1951 (excellent fiction).

Ziegler, K., 'Pantheon', in Pauly-Wissowa, *Realencyclopädie der klassischen Altertumswissenschaft*, 18.3, 1949, cols. 697–747.

NOTES

[Full titles, when not given, will be found above in the Bibliography; **bold** numbers indicate page references.]

12 Hadrian: A. Garzetti, *From Tiberius to the Antonines*, London, 1974 (chapter 10 and Appendices); B. d'Orgeval, *L'empereur Hadrien*, Paris, 1950, list of public works, pp. 269–76; and architecture, Kähler (1950), Introduction and Part IV; Yourcenar, with critical bibliography; W. Weber, *Untersuchungen zur Geschichte des Kaisers Hadrianus*, Leipzig, 1907.

poetry: *Minor Latin Poets*, in the Loeb collection.

quotation: *Scriptores Historiae Augustae: Hadrian* 14.11.

willfulness: ibid., 19.9 and 20.4; cf. 19.2: 'he built something in almost every city'. *Apparent*, because as Prof. W. L. Loerke kindly pointed out, in a helpful elucidation of the inscription, 'good' emperors such as Augustus and Hadrian preserved the names of original donors when rebuilding.

13 Agrippa's Pantheon: de Fine Licht, pp. 172–9. Agrippa: T. Rice Homes, *The Architect of the Roman Empire*, Oxford, 1928; M. Reinhold, *Marcus Agrippa*, Geneva and New York, 1933; Boëthius and Ward-Perkins, pp. 185 and 564; F. W. Shipley, *Agrippa's Building Activities in Rome*, St Louis, 1933, pp. 55–65.

brick-stamps: H. Bloch, *I bolli laterizi e la storia edilizia romana*, Rome, 1947, reprinted from the *Bolletino communale* (see Cerasoli) 64, 65 and 66, 1936–8, and 'The Roman Brick Industry and its Relation to Roman Architecture', *Journal of the Society of Architectural Historians*, 1, 1941, pp. 3–8.

annual consuls: listed in A. Samuel, *Greek and Roman Chronology*, Munich, 1972 (=*Handbuch der Altertumswissenschaft* 1.7), pp. 253–76, and in handbooks of Roman history.

brick-stamps in the Pantheon: MacDonald, p. 96, notes 5 and 6.

14 Temple of Venus and Rome: G. Snijder, 'Kaiser Hadrian und der Temple der Venus und Rome', *Jahrbuch des deutschen archäologischen Institut*, 55, 1940, pp. 1–11.

designed himself: Rivoira (1909); MacDonald, pp. 129–37.

those who have held: the long argument about the date of the Pantheon can be traced through de Fine Licht, pp. 180–90 and 286–8, and MacDonald, pp. 95–6 and notes. There is an inscription on the architrave* of the porch that states that the Pantheon was restored in 202, and even this has been used to date the building; good discussion by de Fine Licht, p. 190.

consecrated: John the Deacon, in the *Monumenta Germaniae Historia*, Hanover, 1848, 7.8.20:

> Another Pope, Boniface, asked the same [Emperor Phocas, in Constantinople] to order that in the old temple called the Pantheon, after the pagan filth was removed, a church should be made, to the holy virgin Mary and all the martyrs, so that the commemoration of the saints would take place henceforth where not gods but demons were formerly worshipped.

18 prohibition: *Codex Theodosianus*, 14.14; cf. 14.3.10; p. 775 in the Mommsen and Meyer edition (I owe this second reference to the kindness of Professor de Fine Licht).

Campus Martius: F. Castagnoli, 'Il Campo Marzio nell'antichità', *Atti dell'Accademia nazionale dei Lincei*, 1946 (pub. 1948), pp. 93–193.

Constans II: F. G. Moore, 'The Gilt-Bronze Tiles of the Pantheon', *American Journal of Archaeology*, 3, 1899, pp. 40–43; cf. G. Ostrogorsky, *History of the Byzantine State*, trans. J. Hussey, Oxford, 1956, p. 109; and, for the repairs and restorations made over the centuries, see Cerasoli, Montani, Sanguinetti, Terenzio, and Tomei.

lead covering: Tomei.

bell tower: erected in 1270 according to the inscription to the right of the door, pavement level, porch side [32].

Raphael: T. Buddensieg, 'Raphael's Grab', *Munuscula discipulorum* (=*Fest. H. Kauffmann*, Berlin, 1968).

19 Bernini or Maderno: H. Hibbard, *Carlo Maderno*, London, 1971, pp. 230–31; cf. *Palladio*, 20, 1970, pp. 73–88.

woodcuts, etc.: Egger; Lanciani (1882); A. P. Frutaz, *Le piante di Roma*, vol. I, Rome, 1962; illustrations 9 and 10 here are representative of a large number of views of the building.

porch despoiled: Lanciani (1897) 483–6.

pasquinade: it is well known, certainly, but it may not be genuine seventeenth-century wit; see Hibbard, op. cit., p. 230.

defend the Holy See: de Fine Licht, p. 241.

tombs: Manetti, U., *Il Pantheon di Agrippa e le tombe dei reali d'Italia*, Rome, 1928.

1929–34: Terenzio.

24 proposals: B. Blomé, 'Piazza della Rotunda al Pantheon', *Opuscula romana*, 4, 1962, pp. 1–28.

Ammianus: 16.10.14 and 17.4.13; for Ammianus and art, see R. MacMullan, 'Some Pictures in Ammianus Marcellinus', *Art Bulletin*, 46, 1964, pp. 435–55.

*Lowest horizontal member of an entablature.

27 pre-existing monuments: these, and the Temple of Matidia, are documented and illustrated in Nash.

forecourt: Lanciani (1881, 1882); de Fine Licht, pp. 25–34. Some of the paving-stones were re-used for the ramp and piazza of the Campidoglio, R. Lanciani, *The Destruction and Excavation of Ancient Rome*, New York, 1899, p. 264.

28 arch: Lanciani (1881), section 15.

steps: Lanciani (1881), section 5; cf. Vitruvius 3.4.4.

Egyptian granite: C. H. O. Scaife, 'The Origins of Some Pantheon Columns', *Journal of Roman Studies*, 43, 1953, p. 37.

entasis: G. P. Stevens, 'Entasis of Roman Columns', *Memoirs of the American Academy in Rome*, 4, 1924, pp. 121–52, esp. pp. 144–5 and Fig. 1.

structural strength: I would like to thank Professor Henry Millon for discussing this matter with me. For the view that the bronze was structural, see de Fine Licht, pp. 47–8.

imitation barrel vaults: Vitruvius 7.3.1–3. The upper semicircle visible in illustration 23 here shows where the west aisle 'vault' met the intermediate block.

33 step-rings: developed at least as early as Trajan's time; Rivoira, p. 117; cf. illustration 65 here.

34 Neptune: Nash, I, 196–7; G. Gatti, 'Il Portico . . . e La Basilica di Nettuno', *Atti III* (see D'Ossat), pp. 61–74.

equal height: following Vitruvius' prescription for round buildings, 5.10.5, and cf. 4.8.3.

35 colored granites and marbles: F. Corsi, *Delle pietre antiche*, Rome, 1845, pp. 356–7; for ancient marbles, R. Gnoli, *Marmora romana*, Rome, 1971; for the role of color in Roman architecture and in the Pantheon, G. A. Mansuelli, 'Il problema di spazio e colore prima dell'età bizantina', *XVI Corso di cultura sull'arte ravennate e bizantina*, 1969, pp. 267–86.

37 bronze grilles: these openings brought some light to the six niches in the original building; most of the niches are now roofed over at the first cornice level [69].

38 rosette: W. J. Anderson and others, *The Architecture of Ancient Rome*, 2nd edition, London, 1927, p. 81.

concrete: MacDonald, chapter 7 and references on p. 201; Lugli; Blake.

42 Roman order: MacDonald, pp. 154–66.

43 decrease regularly: Lugli, I, p. 439; Terenzio.

44 circularity in architecture: C. E. Isabelle, *Les édifices circulaires et les dômes*, Paris, 1855; L. Hautecoeur, *Mystique et architecture: Symbolisme du cercle et de la coupole*, Paris, 1944.

45 Treasury of Atreus: A. W. Lawrence, *Greek Architecture*, Penguin Books, 1957, pp. 59–62.

tumuli and tombs: J. M. C. Toynbee, *Death and Burial in the Roman World*, London, 1971, chapters 5 and 6.

similar structures: G. C. Picard, *Les trophées romains*, Paris, 1957 (= *Bibliothèque des écoles françaises d'Athènes et de Rome*, 187), under Adamklissi, La Turbie, etc.

Lysicrates: Lawrence, op. cit., p. 187.

Augustus and Hadrian: Nash.

Delphi and Epidauros: Lawrence, op. cit., chapter 17.

round temple by the Tiber; D.E.Strong and J.B.Ward-Perkins, 'The Round Temple', *Papers of the British School at Rome*, 28, 1960, pp. 7–33; F.Rakob and W.-D.Hielmayer, *Der Rundtempel am Tiber in Rom*, Rome, 1973.

Tivoli: C.F.Giuliani, *Tibvr, pars prima*, Rome, 1970 (=*Forma italiae*, I.7), pp. 119–43.

49 Samothrace: K.Lehmann, *Samothrace, A Guide*, 4th edition, Locust Valley, N.Y., 1975; Lawrence, op. cit., 187–8. Professor Phyllis Lehmann kindly discussed Greek circular buildings with me.

Nisa: G.A.Pugachenkova, *Puti razvitiia arkitektury Turkmenistana*, Moscow, 1958, 100–103. I owe this reference to the kindness of Professor Philip Lozinski.

50 Temple of Mercury: A.Maiuri, 'Terme di Baia', *Bolletino d'Arte*, 36, 1951, pp. 359–64; MacDonald, p. 11.

Pompeii: de Fine Licht, pp. 211–16.

Pozzuoli: A.Maiuri, *I campi flegrèi*, 3rd edition, Rome, 1958, pp. 24–31.

54 Golden House: MacDonald, chapter 2.

Krautheimer: R.Krautheimer, 'Sancta Maria Rotunda', in his *Studies in Early Christian, Medieval, and Renaissance Art*, New York and London, 1969, p. 111; this article appeared originally in *Arte del primo millennio*, Turin, 1953, pp. 23–7.

loved novelty: G.Charles-Picard, *Augustus and Nero*, London, 1966, chapter 4, controversial, stimulating; MacDonald, pp. 41–3.

Ward-Perkins: J.B.Ward-Perkins, 'Nero's Golden House', *Antiquity*, 30, 1956, p. 219.

57 Markets of Trajan: MacDonald, chapter 4.

Titus: Nash; G.Zorzi, *I disegni delle antichità di Andrea Palladio*, Venice, 1959, pp. 65–6, and Plates 89–95. The ruins Palladio saw are largely gone, and it is difficult to tell if what he recorded was of Titus' time or later.

58 villa at Tivoli: Kähler (1950); S.Aurigemma, *Villa Adriana*, Rome, 1961: E.Clark, *Rome and a Villa*, New York, 1962, Part II; cf. *Scriptores Historiae Augustae: Hadrian*, 26.5.

60 Agrippa's Pantheon: see note to p. 13.

Pliny: *Natural History*, 36.38.

official Augustan architecture: Boëthius and Ward-Perkins, chapter 7.

late 1890s: Beltrami (1898).

62 locate the caryatids: de Fine Licht, p. 288.

Roman foot: F.Hultsch, *Griechische und römische Metrologie*, Berlin, 1882, pp. 74–9; A.E.Berriman, *Historical Metrology*, New York, 1953, pp. 121–3.

63 imperial eagle: kindly conveyed to me by Dott. Lucos Cozza, who studied the pediment cramp holes. Cf. de Fine Licht, pp. 46–7; and the remains of the pediment of the Temple of Sulis-Minerva at Bath, I.A.Richmond and J.M.C.Toynbee in the *Journal of Roman Studies*, 45, 1955, pp. 97–105. Wreaths sometimes appear in the

pediments of temples represented on coins, as for example on a fourth-century issue showing Hadrian's Temple of Venus and Rome; D.F.Brown, *Temples of Rome as Coin Types*, New York, 1940 (=*Numismatic Notes and Monographs*, 90), Plate IX.6.

67 model: C.Chipies, 'Model of the Pantheon', *American Architect*, 33, 1891, pp. 137–8.

68 Largo Argentina: Nash; G.Marchetti-Longhi, *L'area sacra del Largo Argentina*, Rome, 1960. Tholos diameter about 50 feet. See *The Athenian Agora, A Guide*, 2nd edition, Athens, 1962, pp. 45–7 and Plate III, for an uncolumned tholos (originally fifth century B.C.) to which a porch was added in Augustan times.

150 feet: I owe the suggestion of taking the diameter between niche column centers to Professor Peter Collins.

Leonardo: from Vitruvius, 3.1; cf. R.Wittkower, *Architectural Principles in the Age of Humanism*, 3rd edition, London, 1962, pp. 13–19.

70 sympathy: MacDonald, pp. 43–5.

Roman theaters: if the lower zone of the rotunda interior were made straight in plan, it would be very much like the theater-inspired Septizodium in Rome; Nash. Cf. de Fine Licht, Fig. 221, and M. Lyttleton, *Baroque Architecture in Classical Antiquity*, London, 1974.

76 Greek lands: Ziegler.

quotation: Dio Cassius 53.27.2–4.

77 confirmed: Pliny 9.58 (121).

78 such programs: conveniently in D.Earl, *The Age of Augustus*, New York, 1968.

formal worship: idem., pp. 166–76.

Forum of Augustus: P.Zanker, *Forum Augustum, das Bildprogramm*, Tübingen, 1968.

'things accomplished'; the famous *Res Gestae*, fairly complete in both Latin and Greek on the walls of a temple in Ankara; English translation by P.A.Brunt and J.M.Moore, London, 1967. 'For power he had sacrificed everything; he had achieved the height of all mortal ambition and in his ambition he had saved and regenerated the Roman People.' So R.Syme, *The Roman Revolution*, Oxford, 1939, p. 534.

82 same spirit: D.Earl, op. cit.

84 Augustan model: Garzetti (p. 138, above), p. 434; M.Grant, *Roman Imperial Money*, London, 1954, pp. 205–7.

Hellenistic principles: as at Kos, Didyma, etc.; conveniently seen in C.M.Havelock, *Hellenistic Art*, London, 1971.

85 high vertical features: Professor Frank E.Brown called my attention to the similarity between the Pantheon façade and the way the Temple of Mars Ultor backs against the Forum wall, and I want to thank him for generously allowing me to make use of the idea here.

excavation: C.Ricci in *Capitolium*, 6, 1930, pp. 157–89; G.Lugli, *Roma antica, il centro monumentale*, Rome, 1946, pp. 258–69.

86 classical tradition: D.E.Strong, 'Some Observations on Early Roman Corinthian', *Journal of Roman Studies*, 53, 1963, pp. 73–84.

88 atrium house : Boëthius and Ward-Perkins, pp. 154–9.
syncretism : J. Ferguson, *The Religions of the Roman Empire*, London, 1970, chapter 12.
Mithraism and Christianity : ibid., chapter 7.
89 quotation : *Giessen Papyri*, 3, quoted by Ferguson, op. cit., p. 49.
91 judicial court : Dio Cassius 69.7 ; '[Hadrian] transacted with the aid of the Senate all the important and most urgent business, and he held court with the assistance of the foremost men, now in the palace, now in the Forum or the Pantheon or various other places, always being seated on a tribunal, so that whatever was done was made public.'
92 dome of heaven : E. B. Smith, *Architectural Symbolism of Imperial Rome and the Middle Ages*, Princeton, 1956, chapter 2 ; K. Lehmann, 'The Dome of Heaven', *Art Bulletin*, 27, 1945, pp. 1–27, reprinted in W. E. Kleinbauer, ed., *Modern Perspectives in Art History*, New York, 1971 ; cf. *Journal of the Society of Architectural Historians*, 29, 1970, p. 263, where W. C. Loerke suggests the Pantheon was a temple of the cosmos.
Shelley : letter of 23 March 1819 to Thomas Love Peacock (*The Letters of Percy Bysshe Shelley*, ed. F. L. Jones, Oxford, 1964, vol. 2, pp. 87–8).
Brown : (1961), p. 35.
Yourcenar : pp. 164–5.
Trajan's column : R. Bianchi Bandinelli, *Rome, the Centre of Power*, London, 1970, chapter 5.
94 truly large : the rotunda interior has a volume of some 70,000 cubic m., about twice that of the Guggenheim Museum in New York City.
95 cannot be attempted : there are various materials in de Fine Licht, pp. 249–51 and 317–18 ; M. Pallottino, *The Meaning of Archaeology*, New York, 1969 ; C. L. V. Meeks, *Italian Architecture 1750–1914*, New Haven, 1966 ; Krautheimer, see note to p. 54 ; P. Sanpaolesi, 'Strutture a cupola autoportanti', *Palladio*, 21, 1971, 3–64 ; and S. Bordini, 'Bernini e il Pantheon', *Quaderni dell'Istituto di Storia dell'Architettura*, 79–84, 1967, pp. 53–84, esp. pp. 80–84.
exciting potential : J. B. Ward-Perkins, 'The Italian Element in Late Roman and Early Medieval Architecture', *Proceedings of the British Academy*, 33, 1947, pp. 163–94.
98 bath complexes : D. Krencker, *Die Trierer Kaiserthermen*, Augsburg, 1929 (collects data from around the Empire).
Pergamon : O. Deubner, *Das Asklepieion von Pergamon*, Berlin, 1938 ; Boëthius and Ward-Perkins, pp. 388–9 and 393–5.
Ostia : C. C. Briggs, 'The "Pantheon" of Ostia . . .', *Memoirs of the American Academy in Rome*, 8, 1930, pp. 161–9.
100 Temple of Romulus : Nash ; Boëthius and Ward-Perkins, pp. 505 and 509.
Scotland : M. J. T. Lewis, *Temples in Roman Britain*, Cambridge, 1966, pp. 78–9, and *Antiquity*, 48, 1974, pp. 283–7.
S. Andrea : J. Toynbee and J. Ward-Perkins, *The Shrine of St Peter and the Vatican Excavations*, London, 1956, p. 11 ; the S. Andrea design

appears to be similar to that of the Mausoleum of Helena (fourth century).

101 Gordians: Boëthius and Ward-Perkins, pp. 503–5; A.Frazer, 'The Porch of the Tor de' Schiavi at Rome', *American Journal of Archaeology*, 73, 1969, pp. 45–8.

Split: R.Adam, *Ruins of the Palace of the Emperor Diocletian*, London, 1764; Crema (1959), 624–6.

Maxentius: A.Frazer, 'The Iconography of the Emperor Maxentius' Buildings in Via Appia', *Art Bulletin*, 48, 1966, pp. 385–92.

104 Minerva Medica: Boëthius and Ward-Perkins, pp. 509–11; M.Stettler, 'St Gereon in Köln und der sogenannte Tempel der Minerva Medica in Rom', *Jahrbuch des römisch-germanischen Zentralmuseums Mainz*, 4, 1957, pp. 123–8. Cf. illustration 102, lower right-hand corner, the so-called 'Temple of Telesphoros', undated.

105 preserved: J.B.Ward-Perkins, 'Memoria, Martyr's Tomb and Martyr's Church', *The Journal of Theological Studies*, 17, 1966, pp. 20–37, and 'Imperial Mausolea and Their Possible Influence on Early Christian Central-Plan Buildings', *Journal of the Society of Architectural Historians*, 25, 1966, pp. 296–9; cf. F.W.Deichmann, 'Untersuchungen an spätrömischen Rundbauten in Rom und Latium', *Archäologischer Anzeiger*, 56, 1941, pp. 733–48.

double-shell: W.L.MacDonald, *Early Christian and Byzantine Architecture*, New York, 1962.

Holy Sepulchre: R.Krautheimer, *Early Christian and Byzantine Architecture*, Penguin Books, 1965, pp. 49–51; L.E.C.Evans, The Holy Sepulchre', *Palestine Exploration Quarterly*, 100, 1968, pp. 112–36; C.Coüasnon, *The Church of the Holy Sepulchre in Jerusalem*, London, 1974.

S.Costanza: Krautheimer, op. cit., pp. 41–4; M.Stettler, 'Zur Rekonstruktion von S. Costanza', *Römische Mitteilungen*, 58, 1943, pp. 76–86.

Orthodox Baptistery: S.Kostof, *The Orthodox Baptistery of Ravenna*, New Haven, 1965.

107 Constantinople: there was a chamber called the Pantheon in the Great Palace of the Byzantine Emperors; R.Guilland, *Études de topographie de Constantinople byzantine*, Berlin, 1969, vol. I (=Berliner byzantinistische Arbeiten, 37), pp. 124–6.

108 Alcuin: quoted in M.R.Scherer, *Marvels of Ancient Rome*, New York, 1955, p. 3; for the period, see P.Llewellyn, *Rome in the Dark Ages*, London, 1970.

Mirabilia: Armellini, chapter II and Bibliography; L.Schudt and O.Pollak, *Le guide di Roma: Materialen zu einer Geschichte der römischen Topographie*, Vienna, 1930.

Peruzzi: the drawing is in the Biblioteca Communale Ariostea in Ferrara; H.Burns, 'A Peruzzi Drawing in Ferrara', *Mitteilungen des kunsthistorischen Institutes in Florenz*, 12, 1965–6, pp. 245–70. For other Renaissance drawings of the Pantheon, see Egger, and also Lanciani (1882), pp. 340–45.

110 Palestrina and Tivoli: Boëthius and Ward-Perkins, pp. 140–3; and
   C.F.Giuliani, *Tibvr, pars prima*, Rome, 1970 (=*Forma italiae*, 1.7),
   pp. 164–201.
111 monuments of the past: see T.Buddensieg's 'Criticism and Praise of
   the Pantheon in the Middle Ages and the Renaissance', *Classical
   Influences of European Culture*, ed. R.R.Bolgar, Cambridge, 1971,
   pp. 259–67.
   Raphael: E.G.Holt, ed., *A Documentary History of Art*, I, New York,
   1957, pp. 289–96; for his Pantheon drawings, see Buddensieg,
   op. cit., p. 266, and MacDonald, p. 117.
   quotation: adapted from Holt, vol. II, 1959, pp. 41–3; cf. T.Budden-
   sieg, 'Das Pantheon in der Renaissance', *Sitzungsberichte der
   Berliner kunstgeschichtlichen Gesellschaft*, 13, 1964–5, pp. 3–6.
   learned better: R.Wittkower, *Architectural Principles in the Age of
   Humanism*, 3rd edition, London, 1962, p. 5: '. . . the Pantheon,
   which was and remained of course the most influential classical
   building [for Alberti, and other architects after him, regarding
   ideas on centralized planning]'. Cf. Palladio's *Fourth Book*, ch. 2.
112 Bramante: he seems to have been the first to revive ancient vault-
   coffering, in S. Maria presso S. Satiro, Milan, in the 1480s.
   Michelangelo: J.S.Ackerman, *The Architecture of Michelangelo*, vol. I,
   London, 1961, chapter 8. For the Pantheon idea in the sixteenth
   century, M.Gosebruch, 'Vom Pantheon Vergleichlich-unvergleich-
   liches römische Thermenarchitektur und ihre Auswirkungen die
   Baukunst des Cinquecento', *Tortulae* (=*Römische Quartalschrift*, 30,
   1966), pp. 147–68.
   Palladio: J.S.Ackerman, *Palladio*, Penguin Books, 1966; G.Zorzi,
   I disegni delle antichità di Andrea Palladio, Venice, 1959; there is a
   Bolletino . . . Palladio, Vicenza, 1959 ff. The *Quattro libri*, in an
   English version by Isaac Ware, were reprinted in New York in
   1965: Andrea Palladio, *The Four Books of Architecture*.
114 baths: Zorzi, op. cit., p. 64.
   ruins he restored: Palestrina, for example; Zorzi, op. cit., Plate 204.
   'irreverent': Ackerman, op. cit., p. 137.
   present opinion: Hibbard, *Maderno*, 1971, p. 231; Ackerman, op.
   cit., p. 138.
117 Vignola: J.S.Ackerman and W.Lotz, 'Vignoliana', *Essays in Memory
   of Karl Lehmann*, New York, 1964, pp. 1–23.
   book: A.Giovannoli, *Vedute degli antichi vestigj di Roma*, Rome, 1616.
119 Bernini: Bordini (see note to p. 95); H.Hibbard, *Bernini*, Penguin
   Books, 1965.
123 hundred faults: Hibbard, op. cit., p. 149.
   Neo-Classicism: H.Honour, *Neo-Classicism*, Penguin Books, 1969
   (especially chapter 2).
   Desgodetz: see the Bibliography.
   Jones: J.Summerson, *Inigo Jones*, Penguin Books, 1966, pp. 35–6.
   Chiswick: N.Pevsner, *Middlesex*, Penguin Books, 1951, p. 35.
   Stowe: N.Pevsner, *Buckinghamshire*, Penguin Books, 1960, p. 259.

124 quotation: Alexander Pope, *Epistles to Several Persons* (*Moral Essays*), ed. F. W. Bateson, New Haven, 1951, p. 136.

Wyatt: J. Summerson, *Architecture in Britain, 1530 to 1830*, Penguin Books, 1970, pp. 457–9. The building influenced Charles Bulfinch directly: B. Pickens, 'Wyatt's Pantheon, the State House at Boston, and a New View of Bulfinch', *Journal of the Society of Architectural Historians*, 29, 1970, pp. 124–31.

Legeay: J.-M. Pérousse de Montclos, *Boullée*, Paris, 1969.

Weinbrenner: H.-R. Hitchcock, *Architecture: Nineteenth and Twentieth Centuries*, 3rd edition, Penguin Books, 1969, pp. 43–5.

Paris: Honour, op. cit., pp. 122–32.

125 Halle au Blé: D. Wiebenson, 'The Two Domes of the Halle au Blé in Paris', *Art Bulletin*, 55.2, 1973, p. 277. The relatively small iron parts were more or less standardized, an important step in the development of modern architectural technology.

The Colosseum, London: H. Honour, 'The Regent's Park Colosseum', *Country Life*, 2 January 1953, pp. 22–4.

Jefferson: K. Lehmann, *Thomas Jefferson, American Humanist*, Chicago, 1965, chapter 12; D. Guiness and J. T. Sadler, Jr., *Mr Jefferson Architect*, New York, 1973. Jefferson envisaged a spherical interior for his Rotunda, in the manner of Boullée, Ledoux, and Le Queux; cf. *Visionary Architects*, Houston, 1968, Plates 28–30, 93, 122, 205, etc.

Italy: C. L. V. Meeks, *Italian Architecture 1750–1914*, New Haven, 1966, pp. 166–90.

bodies: *Washington, City and Capital*, Federal Writers Project, Washington, 1937, p. 235.

famous men: Honour, op. cit., p. 83.

131 Hall of Statuary: *Washington*, pp. 238–40.

Mosta: S. Rossiter, *Malta*, London, 1968, p. 109.

132 despotic: there are many examples, but few more interesting than the projects described and illustrated by A. Speer, *Inside the Third Reich*, New York, 1970, pp. 212–13.

133 Porter: A. K. Porter, *Beyond Architecture*, 2nd edition, Boston, 1928, p. 15.

Michelangelo: quoted by Lanciani, 1897, p. 480.

LIST
OF
ILLUSTRATIONS

[(F) = Fototecta Unione, presso Accademia Americana, Via A. Masina, 00153 Roma: (S) = Smith College Slide and Photograph Collection. Photographs not otherwise credited were taken by the author.]

K. Lehmann, 'Piranesi as Interpreter of Roman Architecture', *Piranesi*, Northampton, Massachusetts, 1961, pp. 88–98; (F).

10. The Pantheon, view by Giovannoli. See p. 145; cf. Lanciani (London, 1897; see Bibliography), p. 484; (F).

11. The Pantheon, plan, drawing by Roland Micklewright after B. M. Boyle.

12. The Pantheon, intermediate block and dome. The restoration of the block pediment can be seen by comparing illustration 9. The low modern roof, center, is over the stairway exit; the west stairway is broken.

13. The Pantheon, dome step-rings. Nearby are leads embossed with the arms of Nicholas V (1447–55) and Clement VIII (1592–1605).

14. The Pantheon before the removal of the twin towers. The bronze letters of Agrippa's inscription had not yet been replaced; (S).

15. Model of the Pantheon area about 300; some of the details are conjectural. See note on p. 19; (F).

16. The Pantheon, with the forecourt restored conjecturally. Drawing by Roland Micklewright after B. M. Boyle.

17. The Pantheon, entrance bay from the interior. The arch subtends more than 180° and is warped in plan because it follows the curve of the cylinder. Compare the entrance arch of Bernini's S. Andrea al Quirinale (see Bordoni, note to p. 143); (S).

18. The Pantheon, tomb of Victor Emmanuel II; from a postcard.

19. Model of the Campus Martius as of about 300; some of the details are conjectural (see note on p. 19). The Pantheon is just above right center; the Tiber is at the top; (F).

20. Plan of the Pantheon area as of about 300, with the known buildings superimposed upon the modern street plan. Both actual remains and data from the Marble Plan are shown (see Bibliography, Ancient Sources); (S).

21. The Pantheon, detail of the porch. The strip in front of the columns marks the area of the steps, and the block at the right the approximate position of the podium projection.

22. The Pantheon, looking up into the porch roof structure. The stone piers, arches, and woodwork would have been unseen in antiquity because of the false vaults that ran north-south. The rising curve of masonry at the far right marks the line against which the false vault 'fitted' onto the real vault of the entrance bay; (F).

23. The Pantheon, upper part of the west face of the intermediate block, inside the porch. The upper part of the great niche vault is visible; above is the semicircle against which the false vault of the aisle abutted.

24. The Pantheon, porch roof and intermediate block. The holes in the stone pediment can be seen, as well as the restored areas of the face of the intermediate block.

25. The Pantheon, rotunda exterior. The arches are the ends of the powerful vaults set radially in the 20 ft thickness of the wall; the piers are between them but masked by the exterior cylindrical wall.

26. The Pantheon, structural diagram. Drawing by R. Larason Guthrie, after L. Beltrami, *Il Pantheon*, Milan, 1898, Plate 4.

27. The Pantheon, terrace at the foot of the dome, north side. The wall at the left begins the series of step-rings at the base of the dome.

28. The Pantheon, section. Drawing by B. M. Boyle. The black portions represent vaults cut through radially. Note the relationship of exterior and interior cornices.

29. The Pantheon, oculus. The bronze sheathing around it appears to be original. The remains of the ancient cornice are in shadow at the top of the opening.

30. The so-called basilica of Neptune abutting the south side of the Pantheon rotunda. The striated· pattern indicates modern refacing; (F).

31. The Pantheon, entrance bay vault and pilaster capitals of the porch. The curve at top center is the extension of that of illustration 22.

32. The Pantheon, the doorway. The top-right plaque is that of Urban VIII of 1632: referred to on p. 94; bottom-right, that which mentions the bell tower of 1270; (S).

33. The Pantheon, theoretical spherical and cubical geometry; cf. F. E. Brown, p. 92 here. Sketch by Roland Micklewright after W. L. M.

34. The Pantheon, light on an aedicula (position 16 on the plan, illustration 11).

35. The Pantheon, pavement and west wall. The center disk of the pavement is approximately at the center of the photograph. From L. von Matt, *Architektur im Antiken Rom*, Würzburg, figure 25.

36. The Pantheon, restored attic zone and environs. The restored portion is over positions 11 and 12 on the plan, illustration 11.

37. The Pantheon, the dome from G. Picard, *Living Architecture: Roman*, New York, 1965, figure 93.

38. The Pantheon, detail of coffering. Notice the obliquity of the bottom surfaces.

39. The Palatine, Rome, detail of the coffering to the south-east of the so-called Hippodrome. The closest surface has been restored, but the moldings lining the recesses are original; presumably the Pantheon coffers were once so molded.

40. Making tile arches over wooden formwork. Kuşadası, Turkey. The temporary woodwork gives the shape of arch desired. To the left, the weight on the pier has been evened by beginning the far left arch. The mason (pith helmet) is bringing both of the arches in front of him up simultaneously.

41. Making tile arches over wooden formwork. Kuşadası, Turkey.

42. Mycenae, the so-called Treasury of Atreus, fourteenth century B.C. From W. B. Dinsmoor, *The Architecture of Ancient Greece*, London, 1950, Figure 13.

43. Tiddis, Algeria, tomb of the Lollii. Tiddis, the ancient Castellum Tidditanorum, is *c.* 20 km northwest of Constantine. The tomb was for the family of Lollius Urbicus (second century), governor of Britain and of Africa, and Prefect of the City of Rome.

44. Le Médracen, Algeria. *c.* 70 km. south of Constantine, it may be the tomb of a Numidian king of the late second century B.C. It is 100 ft in diameter. For this, and a somewhat similar tomb near Algiers, see *Archaeology* 2, 1949, pp. 88–90.

45. Athens, Monument to Lysicrates. The tholos rests on a square base; late fourth century B.C.; from J. Stuart and N. Revett, *The Antiquities of Athens*, London, 1762 ff.

46. The Mausoleum of Augustus, Rome. Built in 28 B.C. The concentric walls of concrete were faced with marble below and probably landscaped in a mound above; (F).

47. The Mausoleum of Hadrian, Rome (Castel S. Angelo). Hadrian's bridge across the Tiber, the Pons Aelius, is in the foreground. The mausoleum, greatly altered since its construction, was built in the late 130s; (S).

48. Epidauros, the tholos. Restored exterior elevation, as of about the middle of the fourth century B.C.; (S).

49. The so-called Temple of Vesta (detail), Rome, by the Tiber. Probably first half of the first century B.C. The cella wall is of marble, the general inspiration Hellenistic.

50. The so-called Temple of Vesta, Tivoli; view by Piranesi (see illustration 9, above). Early first century B.C., with a cella of concrete; partly standing; (S).

51. The Arsinoeion, Samothrace, Greece, section restored; from Conze, *Archäologische Untersuchungen auf Samothrake*, Plate 55.

52. The so-called Temple of Mercury at Baia, from above. The vault and the surrounding roofs have been given a protective covering of cement, but the structure proper is all ancient. The oculus is about fourteen feet in diameter.

53. The so-called Temple of Mercury at Baia, interior. The vault surface was originally sheathed with mosaic.

54. The so-called Temple of Mercury at Baia, section of dome, seen during restoration. From A. Maiuri, 'Il restauro di una sala termale a Baia', *Bolletino d'Arte*, 10, 1931.

55. The Market, Pozzuoli. The tholos is the ring-form in the foreground; the columns belonged to the porticoed court. The original structure was Flavian (late first century A.D.); it was altered in the next century.

56. Nero's Golden House, model of the octagonal atrium. It is in the Museo della civiltà romana (see note on p. 19); (F).

57. Nero's Golden House, Rome, dome of the octagonal atrium, detail. The negative impressions of the wooden formwork boards are visible.

58. Nero's Golden House, Rome, plan of the octagonal atrium. Drawing by B. M. Boyle. Rooms 24, 26, and 29 were barrel-vaulted; 25 and 28 were cross-vaulted (dotted lines indicate vaults or arches).

59. The Markets of Trajan, Rome, interior of a semi-domed hall. This is in form half of a Pantheon, without coffering but with niches of alternating plan. At the top right, the hand-laid concentric rows of stone aggregate can be seen.

60. The cross-vault principle. This sketch, by K. J. Conant, shows only surface, not structure.

61. The Markets of Trajan, Rome, great hall, analytical perspective. Drawing by Der Scutt. The perspective has been forced in order to reveal the design more clearly. A five-foot module was used.

62. The Markets of Trajan, Rome, great hall, vaulting. The vault is original, though damaged here and there. It is entirely supported by fourteen fairly narrow piers.

63. The Markets of Trajan, Rome, great hall, gallery.

64. The Markets of Trajan, Rome, great hall. The stone enframements and mezzanine windows of the shops or tabernae are typical of second-century commercial architecture. The orders are not used at all.

65. The Markets of Trajan, Rome, vault construction. Taken when the Markets were cleared some forty-five years ago, it shows in the foreground the stepped exterior of a semi-dome ; (F).

66. Hadrian's Villa near Tivoli, model showing the Temple of Apollo upper right. The model is on display at the Villa. Lower left, a baroque version of the domed rotunda concept.

67. Hadrian's Villa near Tivoli, ruins of the Temple of Apollo ; view by Piranesi (see illustration 9, above). The windows in the upper zone were made possible by the comparatively small scale of the building.

68. Hadrian's Villa near Tivoli, air view of the remains of the Maritime Theatre and surroundings. Between the outer, enclosing wall and the ring of (stump) columns, there was a barrel-vaulted, circular gallery. The next, sunken, ring was a moat ; from S. Aurigemma, *Villa Adriana*, Rome, 1961 (1962), Figure 49.

69. The Pantheon, interior niche capital. The post-antique ceiling of the niche is visible in the background.

70. The Pantheon, interior niche pilaster capital. The first level cornice can be seen upper right, and the patterning of the marble sheathing to the right and left of the capital.

71. Dougga, Tunisia, fastigium of the Forum Temple. The apotheosis of Antoninus Pius, as an eagle carries him to heaven ; late 160s. Photograph courtesy of Signorina Matilde Mazzolani and the late Dott. Ernest Nash.

72. Ephesos, Turkey, fastigium with a wreath. About five feet wide overall.

73. Palazzo di Giustizia, Rome, fastigium on the south flank (c. 1905). One of the many eagles that have come to nest in Roman fastigia since unification in 1870. This is the kind of effect, though sculpted rather more fully in the round, that has been suggested for the Pantheon.

74. The Pantheon, porch roof from atop the intermediate block. The base for the apex-feature (acroterion) of the pediment is very large, and probably would have carried a large plant-form or figural sculpture, emphasizing the center-line of the composition.

75. Ostia, detail of cornice of theatre with stucco remaining (right). The terracotta core was enveloped in stucco, which was then drafted to look more or less like hard-edged stone.

76. Model of the Pantheon formerly displayed in the Metropolitan Museum of Art in New York. The sculpture is entirely imaginary; the high viewpoint instructive in suggesting what could and could not have been seen from pavement level; (S).

77. The Largo Argentina, Rome, plan of Republican temples. For their location, see illustration 20. From A. Boëthius and J. B. Ward-Perkins, *Etruscan and Roman Architecture*, Penguin, 1970, Figure 63.

78. The Largo Argentina, Rome, detail of Temple B. The extension of the podium during a reconstruction can be seen far left; the block in front of the steps is the core of an altar; (F).

79. Leonardo's interpretation of the Vitruvian man, redrawn by B. M. Boyle. See references on p. 142.

80. Nero's Golden House, Rome, detail of the octagonal atrium. The chamber in the background is no. 28 on illustration 58.

81. The Pantheon, interior, seen from the west transverse niche. The free-standing columns in front of the apse are visible at the right; from J. Durm, *Die Baukunst der Etrusker: Die Baukunst der Römer*, Stuttgart, 1905, Figure 645, after E. Isabelle, *Les Édifices circulaires et les dômes*, Paris. 1855: (S).

82. Sabratha, Libya, model of the theatre stage-building (Photograph. Gabinetto Fotografico Nazionale, Rome).

83. S. Maria in Campitelli, Rome, upper part of the façade. By Carlo Rainaldi, 1662–7.

84. The Pantheon, shadows on the dome coffers (Photograph: Rowland J. Mainstone).

85. Mosaic in the National Museum (Terme), Rome. From a postcard. Second-century; the medallion at the center is about a foot and a half in diameter; black and white.

86. Forum of Augustus, Rome, model. (Photograph: New York University.)

87. Forum of Augustus, Rome, plan. The Forum of Julius Caesar adjoined at the west corner and was at right angles to the Augustan enclosure. From E. Lundberg, *Arkitekturens Formspråk*, Stockholm, 1951, p. 429; redrawn by Ian Stewart.

88. Forum of Augustus, Rome, marblework. This is in the east corner of the room at the end of the north stoa.

89. Forum of Augustus, Rome, pilaster. Upper part of the left pilaster in illustration 88; colored marble; the mitered capital at 90° to it has fallen.

90. Forum of Augustus, Rome, exedra. The southeast curve, shorn of its facing and much marked by the various structures that from time to time were erected against it.

91. Forum of Augustus, exedra niches. The northwest curve, partly restored, where statues of members of the Julian house stood.

92. Forum of Augustus, Rome, plan showing probable locations of statues. From P. Zanker, *Forum Augustum, das Bildprogramm*, Tübingen, 1968, by permission of the publisher, Verlag Ernst Wasmuth; redrawn by Ian Stewart.

93. Forum of Augustus, Rome, the great wall behind the Temple of Mars Ultor. The line of large beam-holes was for the cella roof structure; the steps center (modern) are those in front of the cella apse; and the standing columns right are part of the southeast external colonnade of the Temple, whose cella walls stand in part to the left (restored) and right of center.

94. Forum of Augustus, Rome, remains of the Temple of Mars Ultor. The dark patch in the middle of the steps, left, is where the altar stood.

95. Forum of Augustus, Rome, caryatids and relief sculpture from a stoa attic; from A. Boëthius and J. B. Ward-Perkins, *Etruscan and Roman Architecture*, Penguin, 1970.

96. Forum of Augustus, Rome, coffering of the temple of Mars Ultor. Between the columns of illustration 93, right; (S).

97. The Pantheon, view through the bronze doors.

98. The Pantheon, Rome, dome and oculus. The candles are on the altar.

99. Trajan's column, Rome. St Peter's statue is of the 1580s. In the distance is the top of the Colosseum; between it and the column, part of the great wall of the Forum of Augustus; far left, the beginnings of Trajan's Markets. From L. von Matt, *Architekture in antiken Rom*. Würzburg, figure 30.

100. The so-called Temple of Diana, Baia, of Hadrianic date; presumably a hall in a bath building. Half of the vault, which is slightly elliptical in section, has fallen; cf. the shape of the so-called Treasury of Atreus (illustration 42).

101. Model of the Baths of Caracalla, Rome, early third century (see note on p. 19). The rotunda was *c.* 110 feet in diameter.

102. The Sanctuary of Asklepios, Pergamon, Turkey, model. From O. Deubner, *Das Asklepieion von Pergamon*, Berlin, 1938.

103. The Temple of Asklepios, Pergamon, Turkey, remains of the rotunda wall and apse. Carefully fitted stonework in the Greek and Hellenistic tradition, strengthened with iron cramps set into the stones with lead.

104. The Round Temple at Ostia, plan. From Briggs (see note to p. 98).

105. The Round Temple at Ostia, restored view. From Briggs (see note to p. 98).

106. The so-called Temple of Romulus, Rome. Only the lower part of the curved wall of the entrance court remains. The column, right, was one of two that stood in front of a flanking, apsidal hall; this scheme was repeated symmetrically on the left.

107. S. Andrea by St Peter's, Rome. From Maerten van Heemskerck's *Roman Sketchbook*, 79D 2a. fol. 7r.; by permission of the Kupferstichkabinett, Berlin.

108. The so-called Mausoleum of the Gordians, Rome. The lower windows in the rotunda lit the crypt; the podium vaulting to the right supported the porch.

109. The so-called Mausoleum of the Gordians, Rome, restored. From Boëthius and Ward-Perkins (see the Bibliography), Fig. 191 A.

110. The so-called Temple of Minerva Medica, Rome. The curved wall in the foreground is one of the very large exedrae added to the original building and shown on the plan (illustration 112); (F).

111. The so-called Temple of Minerva Medica, Rome, model. At the Museo della civiltà romana, E.U.R., Rome. (Photograph: Gabinetto Fotografico Nazionale, Rome.)

112. The so-called Temple of Minerva Medica, Rome, plan. Drawing by B. M. Boyle. The solid black areas indicate the original building of c. 320.

113. The so-called Temple of Minerva Medica, Rome, detail of dome construction. The step-rings in 1942; (F).

114. S. Costanza, Rome. The porch, now gone, would be at the left. The tower-like structure to the right admits light to the outer, lower ring in front of the apse.

115. S. Costanza, Rome, interior; view by Piranesi (see illustration 9, above). The decoration in the cylinder and dome (above the columns) has nothing to do with the original building. The mosaics in the lower ring vault are fourth century; (S).

116. S. Costanza, Rome, plan. The columns around the outer wall, now gone, were part of an open exterior gallery. From M. Stettler in *Mitteilungen des deutschen archäologischen Instituts*, vol. 58 (1943), Beilage 1, redrawn by Ian Stewart.

117. S. Costanza, Rome, part of the interior ring-arcade. The difference in light between the inner, higher shell and the lower, outer one is pronounced. The brickwork has been restored somewhat; the holes are for the cramps that held the marble sheathing to the cylinder surface.

118. The Orthodox Baptistery, Ravenna, interior. The floor is quite a bit higher than the original one. Every other side of the octagon, at ground level, is expanded outward in a niche, in the manner of Minerva Medica. From W.F. Volbach and M. Hirmer, *Early Christian Art*, New York, Plate 140.

119. The Pantheon, from the *Mirabilia Urbis Romae*, ed. I.F. Conti, Albano, 1930, p. 43.

120. Detail from the fresco of *The Departure of St Augustine for Rome*, 1465, by Benozzo Gozzoli. S. Agostino, S. Gimignano. (Photograph: Brogi.)

121. Woodcut view of Rome from Jacobus Philippus de Bergamo, *Supplementum Chronicarum*, Venice, 1490, folio 49, recto; Rare Book Department, Free Library of Philadelphia.

122. Peruzzi: longitudinal section of the Pantheon; from H. Burns, 'A Peruzzi drawing in Ferrara' (see note to p. 108).

123. Bramante's design for St Peter's on a bronze coin by Cristofore Caradosso (Photograph: Trustees of the British Museum).

124. Design for the dome of St Peter's, woodcut from Serlio's *Architettura*, 1575.

125. One of Palladio's drawings of the Pantheon, from *I Quattro*

Libri dell'Architettura, Venice, 1570, Fourth Book, Plate III. The treatment of the rotunda exterior is surely hypothetical. On the right-hand side the bronze sheathing of the beams of the roof support is shown. Palladio did not know, or did not think it significant to show, that the angle of the apex of the pediment on the intermediate block is slightly less obtuse than that of the porch; (S).

126. Villa Rotonda, Vicenza; (Photograph: Dearbon Massar).

127. The chapel at Maser; (Photograph: Dearbon Massar).

128. The chapel at Maser, plan; from James S. Ackerman, *Palladio*, Penguin, 1966.

129. Il Redentore, Venice. Close-to, the block above the main pediment functions much like the Pantheon intermediate block, because the roof above it slants back (it is not a pediment); (Photograph: Foto Marburg).

130. Piazza del Popolo, Rome; view by Piranesi (see illustration 9, above). The churches, by Carlo Rainaldi and Bernini, are of the 1660s and 1670s: (S).

131. S. Andrea al Quirinale, Rome. Compare the incurving walls with those of the Temple of Romulus (illustration 106): (Photograph: Anderson).

132. S. Andrea al Quirinale, Rome, plan. From C. Norberg-Schultz, *Baroque Architecture*, Figure 115.

133. S. Maria dell'Assunzione, Ariccia. The flanking buildings are an essential part of the whole composition, which probably reflects Bernini's studies for the restoration of the Pantheon to what he thought had been its original state; see H. Hibbard, *Bernini*, Penguin Books, 1965. p. 149; (Photograph: Gabinetto Fotografico Nazionale, Rome).

134. S. Maria dell'Assunzione, Ariccia, plan. The flanking buildings are carried tightly around the rotunda and down the steep slope toward the rear, and as they turn they become free-standing walls, stage sets; (S).

135. Lord Burlington's Palladian bagno at Chiswick, Middlesex. The porch is very much like that shown in Palladio's Plate XXXI in the *Quattro libri* (see note to p. 112); (S).

136. The Pantheon in the park at Stourhead, 1753–4; see K. Woodbridge, *Landscape and Antiquity*, Oxford, 1970 (photograph: K. Woodbridge).

137. The Pantheon, London. The lower zones are directly related to the Hagia Sophia in Constantinople, fairly accurate views of which were available as early as the seventeenth century, for example in W.J. Grelot, *A Late Voyage to Constantinople*, trans. J. Philips, London, 1683, Fig. VIII, p. 121; painting by William Hodges, Temple Newsam, Leeds.

138. The Hedwigskirche, Berlin. From P. O. Rare, *K. F. Schinkel*, p. 366, no. 232.

139. The Anatomy Theatre, École de Médecine, Paris. Engraving after Jacques Gondouin, from Poulleau's *Description des écoles de chirurgie*, 1780. Gondouin designed the building in 1765. It was built 1769–75.

140. Design for the Opéra, Paris. By E. L. Boullée, c. 1780. Paris, Bibliothéque Nationale.

141. Design for a temple to 'La Sagesse Suprême'. By J. J. Le Queux, 1794. Paris, Bibliothèque Nationale.

142. Interior of the Halle au Blé. Paris, showing the second dome, 1803–13. By F. J. Bélanger. (Photograph by courtesy of Prof. Dora Wiebenson.)

143. Interior of the Colosseum, Regents Park, London. Designed by Decimus Burton 1823–7. Victoria and Albert Museum, London. (Photograph: Victoria and Albert Museum, Crown copyright.)

144. The Library Rotunda, University of Virginia, Charlottesville. Designed by Jefferson and built 1817–26. The interior has been restored to its original (spherical) proportions for 1976; (S).

145. S. Simeone Piccolo, Venice. (Photograph: Alinari.)

146. S. Carlo al Corso, Milan; (S).

147. S. Francesco di Paolo, Naples; (S).

148. S.Francesco di Paolo, interior. (Photograph: Alinari.)

149. The Tempio, Possagno. (Photograph: Alinari.)

150. St Mary, Mosta, Malta. The internal diameter of the rotunda is about 122 feet, and the rotunda walls are nearly 30 feet thick. There are eight niches (including the entrance bay and a deep apse) on the interior.

151. St Mary, Mosta, Malta, detail of the dome. It is said to have been erected without supporting woodwork; that is, that the stones were keyed and fitted together in the manner of horizontal arches, so that each ring was self-supporting.

152. Monticello, Charlottesville, Virginia, designed by Jefferson; (S).

153. The Church of the Immaculate Heart of Mary, Rome. An equal-armed cross intersects the rotunda; the dome has not been built.

154. The Church of Divine Wisdom at the University, Rome. The plan of the rotunda is elliptical.

INDEX